DESIGN CAREER

STEVEN HELLER
LITA TALARICO
DESIGN
CAREER

PRACTICAL KNOWLEDGE FOR
BEGINNING ILLUSTRATORS
AND GRAPHIC DESIGNERS

VNR VAN NOSTRAND REINHOLD
_____ *New York*

Printed in the United States of America

Designed by Seymour Chwast

Van Nostrand Reinhold
115 Fifth Avenue
New York, New York 10003

Van Nostrand Reinhold (International) Limited
II New Fetter Lane
London EC4P 4EE, England

Van Nostrand Reinhold
480 La Trobe Street
Melbourne, Victoria 3000, Australia

Macmillan of Canada
Division of Canada Publishing Corporation
164 Commander Boulevard
Agincourt, Ontario M1S 3C7, Canada

16 15 14 13 12 11 10 9 8 7 6 5 4 3 2

Library of Congress Cataloging-in-Publication Data

Heller, Steven.
    Design career.

    Bibliography: p.
    Includes index.
    1. Graphic arts—Vocational guidance—United States.
2. Commercial art—Vocational guidance—United States.
I. Talarico, Lita   II. Title.
NC998.5.A1H4   1987   741.6'023'73   87-8104
ISBN 0-442-23263-2

CONTENTS

ACKNOWLEDGMENTS

Thanks to Julie Lasky at Van Nostrand Reinhold for her painstaking editing and invaluable suggestions and guidance.

Thanks also to Dorothy Spencer and Linda Venator at Van Nostrand Reinhold; Kevin Gatta for his design; Anne Kerman for additional research; Sarah Jane Freymann, our agent; and to all those whom we interviewed for this book.—S.H. & L.T.

According to Department of Labor statistics, more young people are entering the graphic arts professions than ever before, making this a very competitive but still comparatively accessible field. That you have bought this book obviously means that you are interested in, if not intent on, a career in the applied graphic arts. But it also suggests that you may not yet be clear about the direction in which to go. You have probably chosen between illustration and graphic design already; perhaps you have decided to give them both a try. But you probably have not decided specifically how or where to practice, and you may have the following questions:

Should I freelance or get a staff job?

Should I open an outside studio or work at home?

How much experience is necessary before I can enter the professional world?

This book will help answer the questions regarding your career choices and business directions. It will not teach you how to be a good illustrator or graphic designer, but it will give you good information about the basics. Before any questions can be answered, however, a brief introduction to the applied arts is in order. Those of you who are seniors in or graduates of an art school or university graphic arts department may already know that the field is diverse, but do you know to what extent? And those of you who are contemplating a career change from some other profession into the graphic arts may find that the possibilities are, at first, overwhelming. The following should clear a path through the labyrinth.

Applied arts is the umbrella term under which illustration, graphic design, art direction, and such support jobs as creating mechanicals and comps, retouching, lettering, typography, and so on are commonly classified. The distinction between the applied artist and the so-called fine artist is the intent behind the work. The fine arts are those in which personal motivation is the single most important impetus. Conversely, the applied arts are commerce-oriented, serving the needs of a client. But do not mistake service for lack of inspiration, imagination, and artistry. The history of illustration and graphic design is one of personal expression, visual personality, and, of course, innovation.

Like medicine, law, architecture, and engineering, the applied arts (once referred to as the *commercial arts*), have many different specialties and subspecialties. It is not unusual for the applied artist to excel either in many of these areas or simply in one of them. After the artist works in two or three different areas, a specialty becomes apparent (for example, a preference for editorial over corporate design). The most profound distinction within the applied arts is the relationship between illustration and graphic design. The following are admittedly broad but no less accurate definitions of the two.

Illustration is the painting, drawing, collaging, or sculpting of an image that decorates, complements, or interprets a text or brief. An *illustrator* is one who conceives and/or renders the image. Illustrations are used in many different ways for different purposes: to embellish a page, to draw attention to a statement, to make a statement, or simply to enhance a design. Among the many forms of illustration are *editorial* (visual representations using realism, symbolism, metaphor, or analogy that supplement or complement a news or feature story); *children's book* (narrative images that usually tell a story); *advertising* (realistic or symbolic representations of a product, or an image used to sell a product or idea); *medical* (precise renderings of internal and external biological organs and functions); *technical* (precise schematic diagrams); *informational* (charts, graphs, or maps); *book* (narrative or symbolic adjuncts to a text); and *book jacket* (realistic, symbolic, or decorative representations of the text). Illustration can be done in sizes ranging from the smallest spot to the grandest tableau, in color or black-and-white, and even in three dimensions.

Graphic design is more difficult to define because it is a broad classification that applies to many different forms of printed communication. But for simplicity's sake we will say that the term suggests the aesthetic ordering of type and image to frame and convey a message. A *graphic designer* is one who understands the techniques, technology, and requisites of the print media, combining this knowledge with skill and taste in the act of visual *problem solving* (the buzz phrase for the process of completing a commission or an assignment). In their vintage book *Graphic Design*, Leon Friend and Joseph Hefter state that the successful graphic solution involves "a knowledge of tradition of the craft, a consideration of the purpose for which the design is intended, imagination, and a control of the requisite skill which will leave the artist free for self-expression" (1936: p. v). Describing his own role, Paul Rand, America's foremost graphic designer, says that the designer "analyzes, interprets, translates. He apprises himself of the new scientific and technological developments in his own and kindred fields. He improvises, invents new techniques and combinations. He coordinates and integrates his material so that he may restate the problem in terms of ideas, pictures, forms and shapes. He unifies, simplifies, eliminates superfluities. He draws upon instinct and intuition. He considers the spectator, his feelings and predilections" (1944: p. 4).

A graphic designer has the knowledge and skills necessary to produce a printed piece from conception through printing. The piece can be a book, magazine, annual report, label, package, brochure, poster, handbill, business card, letterhead, or myriad other things. Graphically designed materials come in many configurations; hence, graphic design includes many different jobs, each requiring a variety of creative and technical skills that are all necessary for a graphic designer to be well-rounded. The following are some of the job titles that a graphic designer can hold.

Art director is one of the more enigmatic titles in the business. The job description in one situation may be quite different from that in another. For example, an advertising art director has a very different role than a magazine art director, whose duties are distinct from a publishing company art director, and so on.

Generally, an art director must have a basic understanding of design and production to make the various pieces of a design puzzle come together. Yet, whereas an art director should always be a graphic designer, not all graphic designers need possess the managerial capabilities of art directors. Sometimes an art director does not actually do hands-on design work, but oversees the work of others. An art director might be an illustrator or photographer, but he or she more than likely commissions and checks the illustration work of freelancers. Of course, unique requirements of specific jobs place varying demands on the art director; the following, however, are some common examples of art director positions.

Corporate art director, a venerable title, and *design director*, a relatively new one, correspond to the highest echelon graphics person on a magazine or in a corporation. The design director is usually more concerned with designing the overall format of a magazine than with its day-to-day implementation, leaving the quotidian design work to the art director. For example, when Milton Glaser was the design director for *New York* magazine and Walter Bernard was its art director, Glaser kept a close eye on the format, consulted on the covers, and saw to the creative changes of the magazine, while Bernard kept the whole operation moving. Another example is Louis Silverstein, who, as corporate art director of the *New York Times*, redesigned its many sections, ultimately giving virtually autonomous control of layout and art assignments to his art directors. A design director for a large corporation (such as CBS Records, Container Corporation of America, or Condé Nast) will often hold a corporate-level position, such as vice-president; will be responsible for many other art directors and designers; and will maintain the standards of quality for that company.

The *magazine art director* maintains the format and pacing of a publication; assigns and oversees the work of freelance illustrators, photographers, and designers; is responsible for the effective running of an art department; and serves as liaison with the editors and production manager. Depending on the size, frequency, and budget of the publication, the art department can range in size from one assistant to many, including designers, pasteup artists, staff illustrators, and more. If the publication is large enough, a magazine art director may have both an *associate art director* and an *assistant art director*. The associate is usually the senior designer, someone with extensive experience who oversees the entire creative production of specific sections. For example, *Time* magazine has an associate art director who handles the news section and another who handles features. The assistant usually has minimal experience and, depending on the size and workload of the operation, will design certain sections or feature spreads or will make assignments. The assistant for *Manhattan Inc.* magazine assigns the art for the "front of the book"—the columns preceding the editorial "well"—otherwise known as the *anchored stories*. The assistant for *Science Digest*, on the other hand, only follows through on the art director's designs.

A *book publishing art director* is usually responsible for the overall look of a specific imprint. The art director may design jackets and interiors, but he or she will also commission work from freelancers. Depending on the size of the company and the number of books on the seasonal list, the art director may employ an assistant art director and various full-time designers. At Random House, for instance, a vice-president of graphic design oversees art directors for the six imprints. Each director in turn has one or two full-time associates or assistants who finalize rough designs and sometimes generate their own.

An *advertising art director* is often teamed up with a copywriter to determine a marketing strategy or a visual direction for an entire project—from text to image. The art director usually answers to a *creative director*, the person responsible for coordinating and overseeing creative work throughout the agency or for specific accounts. Sometimes, as is the case with Gene Federico at Lord Geller Federico and Einstein, the art director is also a *principal*, or partner, in the agency.

In-house art director is not a real title (the person to whom it refers is more likely called *art director*, *director of graphic services*, *director of communication graphics*, or *director of corporate communications*), but it is definitely a real position. Large, medium, and small corporations have art directors on staff to produce anything from packaging and labels to promotional displays and employee materials. While some corporations assign their massive corporate identity systems and annual reports to large outside firms (such as Chermayeff and Geismar, Pentagram, Landor Associates, or Seigel and Gale), in-house art directors handle less critical materials. An art director in this position can be a one-person operation or might be responsible for scores of other designers. IBM's art director uses outside freelancers and staff designers alike to produce the myriad forms, brochures, and catalogs issued annually.

There are many corporate and business design jobs with various titles, based on the organization and needs of a specific company and so too numerous and confusing to go into here. Suffice it to say that in-house art departments require people who design packaging, audiovisual titles, charts and graphs, speech support graphics, signage, and more. Any area that requires both type and an image is fertile ground for the corporate designer.

Many of the titles above are exercises in semantics only. An art director for company A may do essentially the same work as the design director for company B, depending on the hierarchy and managerial organization of the company. Unlike the corporate world, design firms are more deliberate in the use of titles. In addition to the legal titles required of all businesses by state and federal law (that is, president, vice president, treasurer, and secretary), design firms add other levels of distinction. The principal is usually called a *director*; multiple principals are *partners*. Sometimes not all of the partners' names are included in the title of the firm, because some partners were brought into the firm as a reward for loyal service years after the original name was selected, or partners were added as the firm grew. Most large and medium-sized design firms have one or two *senior designers*, people with experience who were either hired specifically for the job or worked their way up through the ranks. They are responsible for ensuring that specific projects are accomplished, sometimes oversee designers who have limited experience, and are more often responsible for the mechanics of a specific job. Since many design firms deal with annual reports, which are all produced during the first three months of the year, most employ temporary or freelance designers and *board people* (mechanical artists) to handle this work. It is not unusual for someone doing part-time or entry-level work to be hired as a designer.

Designers, and sometimes art directors, may be hired as adjuncts to other design disciplines. Architectural and environmental design firms, for example, often require designers for signage (the identification and directional markings in buildings, shopping centers, housing projects, and the like) or other graphics-related jobs. Either the firm will subcontract to a design firm or it will hire in-house people on a project basis.

Increasingly, graphic designers are called upon to do more than two-dimensional print design. Many large and medium-sized graphic design firms have become visual communications firms, engaging in multimedia, not just print, work. Chermayeff and Geismar, Milton Glaser Inc., Vignelli Associates, Rudolph de Harak, and others are regularly commissioned to design exhibitions, showrooms, and retail stores dealing with graphics, displays, furniture, and products. Many young designers and illustrators are also being hired by fashion-conscious companies, such as Swatch or Bloomingdales, to design fabrics, packaging, shopping bags, and other promotions. Today's practitioners are required to be generalists, capable of solving both two- and three-dimensional problems.

Most of the titles apply to full-time employment. However, just as it is possible to be a freelance illustrator or designer, it is also possible to be a freelance art director, which usually means taking overall responsibility for a specific project on a limited basis. In fact, many designers are hired by publishing houses, magazines, or corporations in that capacity. The *New York Times*, for example, hires freelance art directors to design within the existing formats of special magazine supplements. The only difference between a freelancer and a staffer in this context is, of course, security and employee benefits. Before making a career, or simply a job, decision, one should know the various advantages and disadvantages of being self- or otherwise employed . . . which leads us to the purpose of this book.

As authors of a guide for the would-be and young professional designer and illustrator entering the full-time or freelance world, our specific purpose is to help you break in or establish yourself in the field and to perpetuate a marketable or employable presence. We believe that regardless of specialty—illustration, graphic design, or a combination of both—the neophyte is given very little practical information upon leaving school and entering the profession. Of course, there is no substitute for experience, and many of you will learn most effectively from your own mistakes. But the process can be simplified and the number of mistakes minimized somewhat by a thorough reading of this book. Herein are addressed the issues endemic to becoming a knowledgeable professional:

- The advantage of internships while you are still in school
- Getting professional work while you are still in school
- Arguments for and against postgraduate education
- The best first job
- Starting out as a freelancer
- Working at home or in a studio
- Sharing space
- Self-promotion
- Selling your work
- Setting up shop
- Learning about suppliers
- Choosing an artists' representative
- Networking
- Joining relevant organizations
- Financial and legal concerns
- Art versus commerce
- Creating a "visual" personality and establishing a reputation

We have organized the book into three sections. The first, *Designing Your Career*, answers commonly asked questions about career choices and planning; employment possibilities; community participation; and business, legal, and ethical guidelines. The second, *Case Histories—Words from the Wise*, offers some homespun, practical advice from professional illustrators and designers, educators, artists' representatives, and advanced students. These people have met the same challenges, made the same mistakes, and learned the same lessons that you will have to address. A thorough reading may save you some trouble. The third section, *For Your Reference*, is a resource listing myriad illustration and design organizations, annual competitions, postgraduate and continuing education opportunities, and books necessary for a well-rounded reference library.

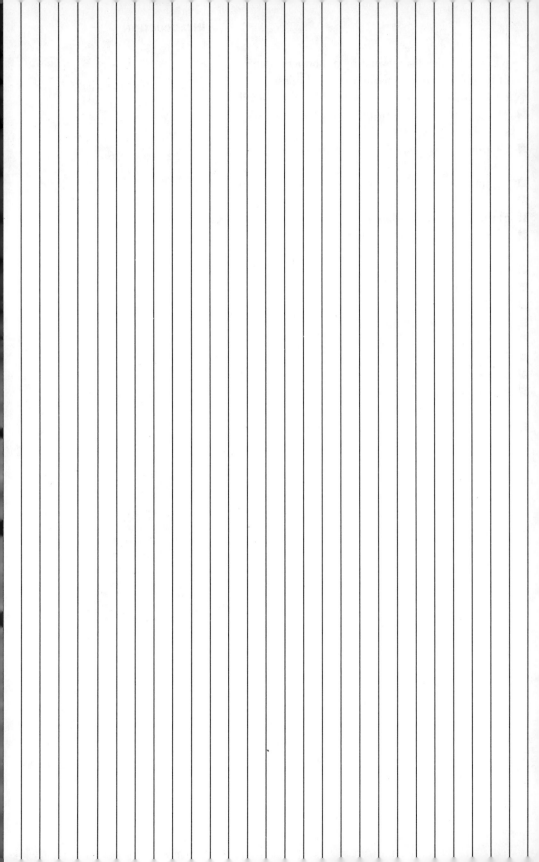

DESIGNING YOUR CAREER

PART ONE

1.
CROSSROADS: CHOOSING AMONG THE ALTERNATIVES

Illustration and design were once happily wed. Indeed, not so long ago, applied artists, like small-town doctors, were invariably general practitioners. The masters of turn-of-the-century poster art, the first real flourishing of printed design, were notable for their striking combinations of type and nonverbal design elements. Today, however, illustration and design are considered distinct branches of the applied arts as a whole, and the venerable graphic arts traditions have all but faded into a mist of overspecialization. If you are entering the applied arts, it is good to remember that an illustrator who knows about page architecture and type is in a stronger competitive position than one who does not, and that a designer who has some illustration skill can articulate an idea better than one who must rely on comp artists.

Sometimes the roads traveled by the illustrator and designer converge; other times they do not. The issue of whether or not to get a full-time job reflects the divergence between paths, because the ultimate benefits of full-time versus freelance employment vary depending on which field is being considered. This chapter is therefore divided into two parts, one for the illustrator and one for the designer. But please do not skip one if you are intent on learning about the other: the information in both may be applicable to your specific needs.

THE ILLUSTRATOR

It must be assumed, although it is not an incontrovertible fact, that anyone who wants to be an illustrator wants to be a freelancer too. Although there are staff illustrators at many corporations (Hallmark Cards is one of the largest American employers of young talent), and a few medium-sized studios around the country that specialize in editorial illustration, like the Don Ivan Punchatz Studio in Texas, illustration is, for the most part, a solitary act, free from the constraints of a boss, supervisor, or foreperson. There are exceptions to the rule, yet most illustrators leaving art school or the university are eager to enter the workaday world. And finding substantive illustration work with the most visible outlet usually means going to New York City to test the waters and make necessary contacts.

The more daring among the neophytes will dive right in: move to New York, find an apartment, perhaps look for a veteran guru, and begin making the rounds of art directors and design studios in the hope that work will come sooner than later. Of this number, some will take interim jobs doing pasteup or running the stat camera at design studios, while others will take unrelated jobs (for example, illustrator and cartoonist Mark Marek worked as a chef at a Soho restaurant at nights so that he could show his portfolio during the day until work began to come in regularly). The more cautious beginners will try to build a client base in their home states and then, secure in the knowledge that they can pay the rent, will venture to New York for a brief pilgrimage.

Although most large cities have at least one or two newspapers, magazines, or book publishers, New York is America's publishing capital. It is therefore the most competitive city as well. But the number of would-be illustrators who come to New York is almost matched by the number of corporations, businesses, and publications that require, if not hunger for, new talent. And while it is true that many high-paying jobs are given to a few "recognized" illustrators, many more low- and medium-paying jobs are given to the newcomer. With enough of these jobs, the neophyte quickly becomes seasoned, and art directors ultimately become aware of their work. As Philip Hays, chairman of the Art Center School in Los Angeles, somewhat humorously but accurately said, New York is the best place if you want to develop an international reputation.

Yet before every young illustrator in America and Canada swarms to the isle of Manhattan, consider some sobering realities. New York is a mecca

3

not only for Americans but for illustrators from Europe, South America, and Asia. Moreover, a great wave of immigrant artists has recently come from eastern European countries, so there is no guarantee that regular work will be available. Be cautious; even a few low-paying jobs a month do not pay the rent, and as the cost of living in New York is very high, the suggestion that one build some kind of client relationship back home is a reasonably prudent one.

Since marketable talent is the only surefire means of immediately securing regular illustration work, you must emerge virtually fullblown from art school with a sought-after or appreciated style to be guaranteed instant success. Vivienne Flesher, Matt Mahurin, and Steven Guarnaccia are among those who made it big in a relatively short period of time because they each had a unique style that was fortuitously in sync with the trends and fashions of the moment. But not everyone develops creatively at the same speed or has the ability to do innovative work at first, if at all. This does not mean that such persons will not make good illustrators. Illustration is, after all, first a craft (many art directors are only looking for a good pair of hands) and, second, an art of accessible imagery and style (which enables the followers to be as successful as the leaders). This means that before making any decisions you should take stock in yourself. Ask the following questions:

☐ What are my strengths?
☐ What are my limitations?
☐ Given the market, how does my work compare with that of established artists? Am I as good as my competition?
☐ How far am I willing or able to go to sell myself and my work?

These questions should not be taken lightly. Judge yourself harshly and seek out as much corroboration from teachers, art directors, and colleagues as possible. If you are *not* good enough or motivated

4

enough, you should know it and move on to something else.

Next you should ask some tough economic questions:

☐ How long can I afford to look for work without any income?

☐ How long can I support myself with low-paying jobs?

☐ What is my financial goal, and how far must I go before I reach it?

Of course, these questions cannot be answered in a vacuum. Perhaps every would-be illustrator should have a certain amount of time in New York to investigate available employment, fee structures, housing, and the cost of living. But once the questions are answered and the move is made, various possibilities become clear. A part-time job might become necessary to tide you over while making the rounds and doing the necessary self-promotions. As Steven Guarnaccia said, it's difficult, given the demands of the marketplace, for the illustrator to take on a full-time job and still be able to practice his craft effectively. But it is also necessary to eat, so if faced with the need to earn a salary, try to get a job at a design studio or other design-related organization. Almost any job will pay the rent, but if you can do mechanicals well, your earning power will be increased. A part-time position would, of course, be ideal, but take a full-time job if that is all you can find. If you are at a design firm, make certain that your employer knows that you are an illustrator; once you are on the job some illustration work may be passed your way. If such a job is not possible, take what you can get and just keep looking. The design field is always in flux, and entry-level workers are always in demand. Check for openings listed in the newspaper and with the Graphic Artists Guild.

If you decide, however, to make a go of it as a freelancer, the best advice is, *do not give up.* Sock away some living expenses, get an answering machine, and make the rounds without fail every

week. Good results may take time. When you start getting jobs, you can change other working arrangements depending on your income level.

If you plan to take the cautious tack and simply visit New York for a limited period to test the waters, do not come for only a few days. Give it some time (three to six weeks is average). Plan your trip carefully. It is a big mistake to call for appointments *after* you arrive in town and expect to be seen. Only a few art directors actually see artists in person, but you should make the attempt anyway. Write letters to art directors, publishers, and illustrators whom you would like to meet. You should include some samples and a résumé. Remember: the illustration game is not like Hollywood; many of your favorite illustrators would be happy to hear from you, meet you, and, if they are impressed by your work, make a few calls on your behalf. Make sure you have a place to stay: a friend's house with a telephone, a short-term sublet, or an inexpensive room at the YMCA.

Be prepared to do some work while you are in town. You may get lucky and be given a rush job, so bring your tools (Brad Holland got his first job from *Avant-Garde* magazine within two hours of getting off the bus from Kansas City). Also bring memorable printed reminders of who you are and what you do.

New York is *not* the only place one can become successful. John Craig, a deservedly busy illustrator who lives in Soldier's Grove, Wisconsin, John Collier, who lives in Lawrence, Kansas, and Robert Andrew Parker, who lives in Cornwall, Connecticut, all prove that illustrators can make their reputations in small towns. It is important to remember that unless you have a very distinctive style or technique, the odds of being a big fish in the New York ocean of illustrators are several hundred to one. If you want to illustrate, make a decent living, and not spend most of what you earn on rent and food, it would be more sensible to stay where you are, or at least to migrate to a less pressured city, like Boston, Atlanta, San Francisco, Seattle, or Chicago. Another option is to work for New York markets through the mails. Thanks to overnight mail services and Fax machines, work can be delivered anywhere within twenty-four hours. An agent is helpful here.

Whether you work in New York, Los Angeles, or Oshkosh, your success ultimately depends on what kind of illustration you want to do and, more important, *can* do. Gear your promotion to that market and go after it with great zeal. Chapter 2 will discuss how to show your portfolio and prepare your samples.

THE DESIGNER

Unless you have decided to practice illustration and design together, the professional realities of becoming a graphic designer are different from those of becoming an illustrator. Many more options are available, not only with regard to the locale in which you can work, but with regard to the variety of work you can get. The following are just some of the areas that offer freelance and full-time employment: design studios; offices or firms; advertising agencies; corporate art departments; editorial art departments; and promotional art departments. Designers are needed everywhere—from the smallest printing concern to the largest multinational corporation.

Unlike the illustrator, whose employment possibilities are decidedly limited to certain geographical areas, the graphic designer can work virtually anywhere—have T square, will travel. Recent "communication graphics" shows held by the American Institute of Graphic Arts (AIGA) and *Print* magazine's *Regional Annual* attest to the fact that exciting, if not innovative, work is coming from many areas of the country once considered design wastelands. Wherever you choose to live or work, design has become a fact of business life. Almost every business eventually requires some

AIGA

7

kind of logo, letterhead, business card, or brochure, and while this has traditionally been a printer's service, graphic designers are now usurping the task. What businessperson needing effective visibility and promotion would choose a standard, often-used layout over a custom-made design? With the increased design sensibility in this country, business graphics offers infinite possibilities for young designers and is a jumping-off point for more significant endeavors.

Equally important, a graphic designer need not be pressured to work as a freelancer. The decision to freelance should be made on the basis of personal preference, temperament, and goals. Design is not a solitary but a collaborative process. Working in a studio or in a corporation—especially at the outset of one's career—is much preferable to starting alone from scratch. Working for someone with expertise, even in an entry-level position, can bring knowledge that school cannot impart, such as the range of available paper, type, and printing suppliers, how to deal with them, how to establish billing procedures, and how to sell a proposal to a client. Furthermore, the printed samples that one can amass through such employment will help to transform a student portfolio into a professional one.

Many different entry-level graphic design jobs are available, from paste-up artist to assistant art director and beyond. There are also countless situations in which these jobs exist—from the all-purpose production studio to the small design firm or office to major corporations. It is helpful to know what your special interests are, but it is not necessary to follow them religiously at this stage.

Usually your first job will be only the initial step and you will be ready to move on after a mere six to twelve months. Regardless, you should try to make an intelligent choice. Although one might reason that any job is better than no job, it is important to know which job will be the most beneficial, rather than the most expedient, for the kind of work you would like to do. Moreover, bear in mind that money is not the most important determinant at the beginning of your career. With this understood, ask the following questions about your prospective employer(s):

☐ What can I learn from a job?
☐ Will my duties give me hands-on experience?
☐ Will I be able to take on more responsibilities over time?

Do not worry too much about the quality of the work that is being produced by your prospective employer. If you respect it, great! If you hate it, do not take the job. If you are uncertain, consider taking it: you will soon learn the difference between good and bad.

If these simple but meaningful questions are answered to your satisfaction, take the job, do your best, work as many hours of the day and night as you can stand, and be flexible, knowing that you will move on to another job or business when you feel you have absorbed all you can. This ad hoc apprentice method is standard. Every employer knows that in time a young assistant will either leave the nest or be promoted to a more responsible position.

Talent is not necessarily the key to initial success in the job market. At the outset, talent is relative and often hard to measure because the beginner's portfolio is usually a reflection of the instructor's strengths and weaknesses. A student portfolio is often a random assortment of problems and solutions that only prove that if the problem is not well-articulated by the teacher, the solution will also be inadequate. Please read the section on portfolios (Chapter 2) and keep in mind that the portfolio is ultimately your passkey. Organize it with all due care and intelligence to show both your *conceptual* and *technical* skills. This means, include as many pieces that show your ideas as those that prove how well you can spec type (read the interviews in Part 2 for tips). The conceptual side is your ability to work imaginatively with type and image, while the technical side is the mechanics of applied art, for example, pasteup, airbrush, lettering, and so on. You should also understand the requirements of the job you are seeking and gear the portfolio accordingly.

Contrary to some pedagogical wisdom, it is advantageous to get your first job while still in school—either during summer breaks or part-time during the school year. A good opportunity for a student is an *internship* at a studio or firm. Although these do not pay, or pay very poorly, one is given invaluable experience in all areas from production to design. An internship usually lasts for a limited period of time, but sometimes leads to more permanent employment with the same firm. Find out about internships by asking your school placement counselor; by writing to the AIGA, Graphic Artists Guild, or local art directors' club; or by contacting the firms themselves. If a firm you are interested in does not offer an internship, try to persuade its principals that you would be an inexpensive asset, albeit a temporary one—sometimes this approach works.

Students should also take advantage of the regular portfolio viewings and visits made by professionals at schools and conferences. Although jobs might not be available immediately, you can make a good impression with your work. A follow-up phone call and, one hopes, a personal appointment often produce good results.

Job placement agencies are not the best resource for beginners. Their clients are usually interested in experienced people. Responding to newspaper ads is more effective, but keep in mind that a good percentage of first jobs come from recommendations. Indeed, the best way to get that first job is the most simple: call as many people as possible. Although a recommendation helps, it is not essential. Simply get names and numbers from the phone book, annuals, or AIGA directory, phone for appointments, then go on as many interviews as possible. Take a representative portfolio that emphasizes the particular area you are interested in. Leave an elegant or clever, but not overworked, reminder of your visit with a résumé. And call back from time to time.

If you are interested in working at a design firm, you should have an idea of the studio or office with which you would most like to be associated. Obviously, everyone wants to work for firms that win the most awards and hence are most widely known. Make a list of whichever you find desirable and call for an appointment. Do not let a gruff receptionist discourage you. Even if the principal will not see you personally, you will probably be able to drop off a portfolio. If you want to choose from a wider range of firms, write for the *Design Firm Directory* (P.O. Box 1591, Evanston, Ill., 60204, $39.00 postpaid). This reference lists two thousand U.S. industrial and graphic design firms and offers detailed information on each.

You may be wondering whether it is necessary to go to New York or any other big city to find a job. The answer to this question depends entirely on your temperament and goals. As stated before, designers can get work anywhere. The highest paying jobs are usually available in the major commercial centers—Los Angeles, Dallas, Atlanta, Chicago, San Francisco, Minneapolis, Cleveland—however, more and more commercial centers emerge each year that need the services of designers. By perusing the list of national professional organizations, art directors' clubs, and AIGA chapters you will see where graphic design is most concentrated (see Part 3, Chapter 3). Sometimes, however, it is more advantageous to start in your home town by working for local merchants: you will be able to collect some good pieces for your portfolio that show what you can do, perhaps on a limited budget, but without too much interference.

If you ultimately decide that going to a major city is the best route, take the bold step—but do not do it awkwardly. Send your résumé and slides to as many prospective employers as possible. Call them for appointments well in advance of your arrival. Make two portfolios, so that if one is under protracted consideration, you are free to show the other elsewhere.

If you are not interested in working for others, you might be considering opening a business as soon as you are out of school. Although starting a design studio is not as difficult as opening a restaurant, it nevertheless requires a certain amount of savvy, which is usually beyond the pale of an inexperienced designer. Most people interviewed for this book suggest that a full- or part-time job is the best way to learn the requisites of design and *design management* (the term applied to the organization and follow-through of a design business). In addition to having regular employment, many designers also opt to do freelance work in their spare time. This methodology is fruitful both financially and experientially and it is much safer than jumping immediately into the melee.

If your goal is to work for yourself, either in a freelance capacity or in a small studio, then build for the future. Develop some ongoing, independent clients before setting out on your own and, most important, attend the various conferences and seminars on design management, such as *How To Sell Design* (Catalyst Educational Systems, P.O. Box 9433, Marina del Rey, Calif. 90292), an intensive one-day course for professional designers, conducted by David Goodman. Seminars and conferences of this type are usually organized once or twice a year in various cities. The live presentations and ancillary tape and written materials are worth the investment.

These are some of the common options for those just entering the field, but there are also many unique scenarios. One always hears stories about the inexperienced designer at a magazine or newspaper who, thanks to a lucky toss of the dice, was made an art director because the person in that position left for better turf . . . or the pasteup person

in a studio who was so talented that she became in-
dispensable almost immediately . . . or the entry-
level designer at an agency who did such exem-
plary work on an account that the client stole him
away to be set up in his own agency. Such scenarios are not apocryphal. They are enacted all the
time.

Having surveyed the career options available to
the neophyte illustrator and graphic designer we
may conclude this chapter with the following observations: The illustrator does better to begin as a
freelancer so that he or she can cover the most
ground in the marketplace. The "generalist" illustrator must slowly build a marketable, yet personally fulfilling, visual identity, whereas the technical
illustrator must develop the requisite skills. This,
of course, takes time and effort, and working on
real jobs is usually the best way to hone those
skills. For the designer, a full-time or regular temporary job with a large or small design firm, corporation, or publication offers the best opportunity for
gaining necessary experience. There is plenty of
time after the first years of apprenticeship to start a
business.

2.
SELLING YOURSELF AND CREATING AN IDENTITY

The term *style* suggests a distinctive conceptual and physical method. For example, an illustrator might have a style that is realistic or decorative, humorous or serious. Style is also a distinctive visual imprint; an illustrator or designer may have a modern or classical style, or an art deco or postmodern style. Not all practitioners have to worry about such things. Many jobs are available for illustrators who render any subject in any manner. Equally, "generalist" designers who solve each problem differently based on the requisites of the assignment have no problems finding work. An individual style is helpful but not a necessity.

Style and *identity* are not the same. Although one's identity sometimes depends on having a particular style, in a more catholic sense, identity is actually how you present yourself as a practitioner, businessperson, and artist. Creating an identity is the process of defining your work in relation to the market, to your colleagues, and to your competitors. An identity is important for all professionals, but crucial for the self-employed. Hence for those who are going to start their own business this chapter will address the following issues of identity:

☐ How to name a business
☐ Stationery and forms
☐ Promotion
☐ Establishing a reputation

Once you have decided on a business direction, you must learn to sell yourself, even minimally. Selling does not mean becoming an applied arts Willy Loman, pounding the streets day after day looking for customers. Rather, it means having the ability to project the image of a professional and convince your clients of your talents. This chapter will cover the basics of selling:

☐ Portfolio presentation
☐ Reminders and promotions
☐ The etiquette of interviews

SELLING YOURSELF

THE PORTFOLIO Regardless of whether you are an illustrator or designer or whether you practice both, there is no tool more important than the portfolio. Anyone even remotely familiar with the profession knows that the portfolio is a calling card and entry key to any kind of full-time or freelance work. It is the first, if not the only, means of creating a professional impression, because most art directors insist that a prospective employee leave his or her *book* (as the portfolio is called) to be scrutinized for a day or two. Where a drop-off policy is in effect, all of your charm, poise, and personality will not do a bit of good; your work will be judged on its merits alone, and the stronger the portfolio, the more likely your chances of getting an assignment or, at least, an interview.

Of course, the quality of your work is the ultimate determinant, yet talent alone does not produce an effective portfolio. Even the physical presentation of your work, though important, is not as important as the *editing process*. Portfolios should not be a catchall for everything you have done during the school term or at interim jobs. Just because you have a printed piece does not mean that you must include it indiscriminately. The editing process ought to begin with the notion that whatever is shown must be the best that you have produced in a specific area. As your samples improve, the portfolio should reflect that progress after you have subjected your work to periodic and rigorous reassessment.

The neophyte's portfolio should include between ten and fifteen pieces and, like any structured book, it should have a beginning, middle, and end. The beginning should be an impressive introduction to who you are and what you want to do. The middle could show other areas of competence or show the lesser, but still interesting, examples of what you would like to do. The end should be as striking as the beginning, so that the viewer is not left with a recollection of your weakest work. Usually only minutes are needed to go through a portfolio, so you will want to make the maximum impact in the least amount of time, leaving the impression that you not only do good work, but that you can present it effectively. The well-edited portfolio will have that result.

Obviously the designer's portfolio is different from that of the illustrator. If you want to present both kinds of work, however, you either can show how the two are integrated, for example, by including book jackets, album covers, or posters in one portfolio, or you can make two distinct books. For those who choose to segregate design and illustration, the following are general guidelines.

The Illustrator   Of the ten to fifteen pieces sufficient for a portfolio, include those that reflect your particular strengths. If you are more proficient with black-and-white, show only black-and-white. Conversely, if color is your strong suit, show only color. The ideal portfolio will indicate that you can work with various media yet that you have a distinctive approach. Too many different styles in one book confuse most art directors. It is good to have one or two originals, but the rest should be reproductions (either stats, c-prints, or transparencies). If you have *good* printed work, include that too.

The book should begin with the most striking image, whether it is printed or not. Other than that, the order is up to the individual. Some illustrators show a printed piece on the left and the original on the right; others alternate between color and black-and-white. Too many just throw in pieces at random, creating the effect of a scrapbook.

If you have a terrific sketchbook, include it. Sometimes sketches appeal to art directors more than finished work.

The Designer   The designer's portfolio should be even more tightly prepared than the illustrator's. A designer is hired for his or her ability to order two- and three-dimensional space, hence, a disorderly portfolio reveals a side of oneself better left at home.

The beginner's ten or fifteen well-chosen examples should include all forms of graphic endeavor —posters, brochures, logotypes, packaging, signage, and magazine or newspaper layouts. These can be comps, dummies, or printed pieces. It does not matter whether you have a distinctive visual persona or not. All that matters is that you show promise.

Those of you who are looking for the first paste-up or board job should include some examples of mechanicals in addition to your design work.

Preparing Your Portfolio   There are so many appropriate ways to package a portfolio that a detailed report would be unproductive. However, by addressing yourselves to the _do nots_ of portfolio presentation the _dos_ will become obvious:

] There are many different kinds of portfolios, including looseleafs, boxes, and suitcases that come in various materials, such as leather, plastic, and fabric. Simply use the one that feels most comfortable. Do not carry your work around in an envelope or paperbag.

] The size of the portfolio is determined by the kind of work you do. Posters obviously take up more space than spot drawings. Do not, however, use a mammoth portfolio. It is unmanageable for the carrier and unwieldy for the viewer.

] There are many different ways to protect and show your work. It can be enclosed in standard loose-leaf plastic sleeves; matted or laminated; or presented on transparencies or slides. The _loose-leaf_ method is good for beginners, simply because your work will be changing rapidly. _Matted_ or framed work invariably looks too precious and usually appears amateurish. Only printed examples should be *laminated;* not only will the pieces look handsome, but this method provides excellent protection. *Transparencies* are effective for showing large work, though some art directors suspect that they are a means of hiding poor technique. *Slides* are effective only when shown in a carousel. Do not include sheets with a hand viewer, as they are cumbersome.

REMINDERS AND PROMOTIONS Reminders and promotions are two sides of the same coin. A reminder is usually a small card or résumé. For illustrators, it can include one or two printed examples; for designers, it is often simply a business card. Promotions, on the other hand, usually show a more inclusive sampling of work and tend to be more conceptual than reminders. While the reminder can be your promotion, ultimately your promotion should be a more complex representation of your work.

Whatever you choose to call it, and whether or not you have an interview or take advantage of a drop-off policy, a card or folder is an important means by which you will be remembered.

The illustrator can make use of a variety of card and folder configurations. The simple *postcard* is the most common and economical to produce. It is also the easiest for the art director to refer to. The illustrator who works both in black-and-white and color is encouraged to have a card representing each approach. A *poster* can be effective if designed and printed well. The odds, however, of having it posted are slight, so posters should be done only if the work is uncommonly striking. A *calendar* allows you to show a variety of techniques or a conceptual range. Large calendars might be hung if they are unique, but small ones are better. A *multisample folder* is often used by artists' representatives and comes in a variety of configurations: in addition to custom-made sizes and shapes, standard folders include the accordion postcard, the four-page brochure, and the single sheet of postage stamp–sized reproductions. The beginner is advised to wait a while, at least until having some good printed pieces, before investing in this sort of reminder. Finally, the *file folder*, in which are placed a number of loose or bound photocopied or printed samples is, for the beginner, the most economical approach. Whatever your choice, do not leave a résumé or a business card without an image. Make sure that you show your best example.

There is an infinite number of imaginative ways to leave a reminder. Among the most unique are small original drawings or prints, which recipients are often reluctant to throw away because an original has inherent value; surprise packets of potpourri whose contents are limited only by your imagination; and slide strips with an attached magnifier, which are, admittedly, more costly than the first two methods described—you will have to do some research to find the least expensive means of producing them. Also take advantage of holidays, especially Halloween, Christmas, and New Year, to send out thematic cards—art directors like saving them.

The neophyte designer's reminder should be more subtle than the illustrator's. A résumé is important and a business card, a necessity. Both should be handsomely, but not overly, designed to represent one's typographical and design sensibility.

Your *résumé* can be typed or typeset (thanks to the new laser printing technology you can get fairly professional, economical typesetting). It should be printed on your letterhead. If you are not certain about your address or telephone number, have stickers, adhesives, or rubber stamps made before investing in stationery. Do not attempt an elaborate design for your résumé. A clean, well-ordered document is more than adequate—restraint is its own reward.

Your *business card* can be the standard size or

19

custom-made, but keep in mind that it should be small enough to be stapled onto a rotating card file. It can be printed in any manner that appeals to you, but should be striking and memorable either in its elegance or outrageousness.

Sample sheets are not necessary in the beginning. However, if you are trying to sell illustration and design talents together, it is best to show samples of posters, lettering, and so on.

Although all reminders are essentially promotions—because they advertise your existence, albeit in a low-key way—not all promotions are reminders. The distinction is subtle yet important. As previously mentioned, the reminder is smaller and usually less expensive to produce, whereas the promotion tends to be more complex and more expensive. Moreover, the promotion is ostensibly a device for hard-sell advertising. While it is advantageous for a beginning illustrator to do a promotion, a beginning designer is advised against it. If the beginner has something to sell, then a promotion is appropriate. If not, he or she should wait a while.

In addition to the specific reminders discussed, there are many ways of promoting oneself in print. The following are some of the most common:

☐ Resource books, such as the *California Workbook*, *American Showcase*, and *RSVP*, enable you to advertise samples in black-and-white or color for a fee (see Part 3, Chapter 2).

☐ Booklets, calendars, and brochures provide showcases for a general sampling of your work. Alternatively, you can use them to present a "conceptual" production in the tradition of the *Push Pin Almanak*, *Push Pin Graphic*, and *Pentagram Papers*—thematic compilations of work based on specific editorial ideas, which exhibit both skill and intelligence. A conceptual production can also take the form of a magazine, short story collection, documentary, or eclectic compendium of art objects. An excellent recent example is *Great Beginnings*, by Mantel, Koppel and Scher, which shows how this design firm typographically interprets the opening passages of great literary works. Another ongoing series is *The Herring Papers*, a quarterly collection of curiosa compiled by Texas-based designer Jerry Herring. If the project is superlative, a printer or paper company might supply the needed services at cost or, better yet, donate them. Suppliers always look for inventive ways to show off their own wares; so much the better if they can do it inexpensively through an existing project.

☐ Promotional gifts are used quite effectively for those who can afford the usually high costs. For example, Push Pin Studios produced a line of Pushpinoff Candies for their current and prospective clients. Although most of you would find it difficult to afford so elaborate a campaign, you should nevertheless investigate the costs of monogrammed pencils, buttons, notepaper, or similar items. Perhaps you will find a reasonable price.

Promotion is ultimately about grabbing a prospective employer's or client's attention in a positive way. Do what you can afford and, above all, make certain that what you have to sell is *worth* selling.

INTERVIEWS Some people become illustrators and designers so that they do not have to deal with math, science, or interpersonal relationships. There is a belief, which holds some truth, that the artist's job can accommodate inarticulateness or shyness. Yet the applied arts are also called the communication arts, and *communication* does not imply merely the language of illustration and graphic design. The applied artist never works in a vacuum; he or she must be able to express ideas verbally as well as artistically. School should be the environment where students develop this skill, but the job interview is often the first important test.

If the portfolio is important as a calling card and vital for establishing credentials, the interview gives the employer an opportunity to see whether or not you are employable, that is, whether you are personable and can get along with others. It also gives you the opportunity to determine whether or not you want to work with the firm.

Sometimes getting an interview is as easy as picking up a phone, so try that method first. Other times it is as difficult as getting Harpo Marx to speak. As a rule, these days, illustrators have a tougher time getting interviews than designers do, because an illustrator usually solicits blindly, whereas a designer responds to a call, referral, or advertisement. In either case, however, various rules should govern the behavior of interviewees.

For example, when you phone to make an appointment and you have not had any previous contact with the prospective employer, do not waste the time of the person on the other end. First, tell him or her the name of the person who recommended that you call, if appropriate, and simply state that you would like to make an appointment to show your work. Do not haggle over the proposed day or time; agree to what is suggested unless it is completely impossible (if you are an out-of-towner, remember that it is best to call two or three weeks in advance of your arrival). Have your appointment book and a pencil beside you and write down the date immediately. Above all, do not try to sell yourself over the phone; offer no information other than what has been requested.

When the day of the interview arrives, be on time, or call if you are going to be unavoidably late. Equally important, be presentable. Do not look like a slob because that is how you will be perceived as a worker. You do not have to wear a suit, but clean clothes, regardless of style, are a must. Although good personal hygiene seems obvious, a surprising number of interviewees arrive without having bathed or showered. Moreover, do not smoke during your interview; you never know who is allergic or simply against smoking. All personal characteristics being equal, let the work do the talking for you; if pieces need an explanation, provide a brief one. Let the interviewer ask you questions, then answer as intelligently and personably as possible.

Whereas these hints apply to illustrators and designers alike, the following cautionary scenarios, originally published in *Print* magazine, were aimed primarily toward the blind phone calls that an illustrator usually makes (with a nod and a wink to the art director as well). All neophytes, however, can learn from them.

The following scenario is not unfamiliar to art directors everywhere.

You are at your desk; the phone rings; a voice asks:

"Can I speak to the art director?"

"I'm the art director."

"I'd like to show you my portfolio."

"Sure. I can see you next Tuesday at 9 o'clock."

"Oh. 9 o'clock. That's a bit early. Can I make it later?"

"I'm sorry," you explain patiently, "but I have other appointments."

"Oh. Well, OK. Let me write that down. Next T-U-E-S-D—"

"I'll see you then," you conclude abruptly.

"Oh, by the way: What kind of work do you like?"

"Why not look at the product?" you say, patience waning. "I've got to go."

"OK. Oh, by the way: What's your name?"

After hurling the phone receiver onto its cradle, you think: If this character is any good, I'll eat an X-acto. Moreover, you begin to wonder why you agree to meet with freelance artists in the first place.

While this particular exchange or one similar to it doesn't occur every day, and usually only with the neophyte illustrator, designer or photographer untutored in the proper graces, it does serve to highlight a major problem in the field: the profession-wide lack of accessibility to art directors by unknown or unrecommended freelancers, both young and old, through portfolio-review interviews—and the reasons for it.

The above scenario illustrates only one of the reasons why art directors prefer the common portfolio "drop-off" method to the more personal one-to-one meeting. A number of other annoying freelancer traits which art directors complain about will be discussed below.

Whatever their complaints, is it nevertheless inappropriate for art directors to avoid direct contact with artists, particularly young ones? Are drop-offs really necessary? Is it reasonable for would-be freelancers to expect art directors to provide the time required to interview them, review their portfolios, and make constructive comments—and to do this for anyone who calls?

Obviously, freelancers would say yes to this. Many I've spoken to feel a *need* for direct contact—are hungry for it—and are chagrined and angry that art directors avoid them as if they were bag ladies or street bums. For freelancers, the drop-off practice is akin to being told: "Drop dead, pal!" Even the most seasoned professional feels shot down when faced with this policy. Of course, the drop-off is a way for the art director to separate the wheat from the chaff in order to save time, but is it fair?

Young artists, particularly, should not have to work in a vacuum, struggling in a profession that is not clearly defined, or perhaps is ill-suited for them entirely. Schools don't always help them in this. And those pre-printed "thank you" notes left in portfolios at pick-up time are rarely helpful, either. It doesn't take a degree in psychology to realize that most everyone looking for work needs to have criticism or encouragement.

It is understood that every art director has time limitations and deadlines. Some simply do not have the budgets or the formats that allow them to buy art, and so for them appointments with artists are

24

senseless as well as frustrating. But too many people—particularly at agencies, design studios, magazines and publishing houses—who are in positions to offer invaluable help do not make themselves available. This is not to say that an art director should see everyone who calls or walks in unannounced—screening can be accomplished over the phone by means of a few simple questions—but an effort should be made to set aside regularly scheduled interview time. Moreover, this should be intrinsic to the job, an accepted part of the daily routine. Of course, the procedures are not written in stone. One need not follow the *New Yorker* magazine's open-house policy, whereby cartoonists file in on two specified days each week. But appointments with reasonable time allotments should be budgeted into the day.

We have all heard the reasons why art directors prefer to see the "book" rather than the person. Sometimes their rationale is heartwarming if unsatisfactory: "I don't like rejecting people" is a commonly heard excuse. Other art directors are more complacent: "I'm just too busy, but if their work is good I'll find them." Some are simply arrogant: "I don't owe students anything. That's the teacher's job. I'm not a teacher." But this last point is a fallacy. Art directors *are* teachers, of sorts. Anyone who has knowledge and experience should be willing to share a modicum of it with others not so professionally advanced. This does not mean one has to squander valuable time or give away secrets, or even assign undeserved jobs. Stated simply, in the vernacular of my forebears, it means a little generosity wouldn't kill you.

Young artists need to be told the truth, or part of it. Frankness couched in compassion is almost always appreciated. Art directors should be articulate enough to speak to an artist in a straightforward, candid manner, and if unvarnished candor isn't possible, to develop a routine of sorts—some key phrases you can call on as required—for dealing with those difficult situations when nothing con-

25

structive can be said about someone's work. Some freelancers I've spoken to who have gotten appointments complain about this or that art director's insensitivity. One should be aware of fragile egos and be able to judge just how much frankness the artist across the table is able or willing to hear.

On the other side of the coin, art directors have valid complaints of their own about would-be freelancers. Almost without exception these concern the artists' deportment or personal style. The following observations culled from my experience and that of other art directors should be taken seriously to heart by illustrators, designers and their agents when showing portfolios, simply because they are what drive art directors crazy, hamper good will and ultimately influence policy. Some comical, yet very real, stereotypes of portfolio presenters follow, which are in and of themselves examples of how not to behave.

The overly effusive (and often disingenuous) artist. Known for continuous blabbering and for such opening statements as: "How are we this morning?" / "Oh, I just love your wall." / "Today I have something you'll *really* enjoy." He or she also tends to stand over the art director's shoulder as the portfolio pages are turned, commenting thusly: "This will fit *perfectly* into your format, it's just like so-and-so's work."

The painfully withdrawn artist. Notable for marked lack of speech, limp handshake, and formless, sunken sitting posture. Any information about this artist or his or her work has to be pried out with precisely the right volley of questions—it's akin to cross-examining a hostile witness in court.

The presumptuously familiar artist. Recognizable from his first telephone call: "Hi, Stevie! I'd like to come over and show you my book today. No, you don't know me, but you *will* like my stuff." And once in the office: "Hi, Stevie! Well, here's what I promised you. What do you think? Fits your format perfectly, doesn't it?"

26

The insecurely self-assured artist. This is a rare bird, but one who flies in from time to time. The classic opening line is: "Hi, I'm the greatest illustrator in the world. Do you think you might be able to use me?"

The fallen fine-artiste. He or she almost always says: "I'm not really an illustrator. I've done *fine* art for years, but now I really need to make some money." In my experience, the work in this case varies from bad to good illustration—but isn't it more satisfying to know the artist being hired is committed to the work rather than doing it just as a job?

The hostile artist. Seemingly an average, reasonably self-controlled interviewee—until you say: "I'm sorry, your work just doesn't fit my needs." Then, hot under the collar, this individual retorts, "Well, you use so-and-so, and I'm much better than that," or, "The work here isn't so terrific anyway." He almost always leaves his card.

The pushy artist (I): "Well, I *know* I could do the job. Yes. I did hear you say what I have here doesn't apply, but even though I don't have any examples to show, I do a very good pen-and-ink. If you give me the job, I'll bring it in tomorrow. Any style you want. No? O.K., what if I bring you some sample pen-and-inks tomorrow morning first thing? No? Well, here's my card just in case something comes up."

The pushy artist (II): "I'll do it for nothing."

There are, of course, sticky situations that emerge from time to time. One art director I talked with, who sees everyone who calls and pronounces her name correctly, told me: "I once met with a man who was given my name from someone in the subway. Instead of telling him right off that I was going on a year-long vacation to the Falkland Islands, I set up an appointment. When he came by I noticed a knife holstered on his belt, and some poorly painted copies of pinball-machine graphics on his portfolio. This did not bode well. His drawings, needless to say, were not good. But I realized he had never talked to anyone about the business of illustration, so I gave him some good advice. He was appreciative, and I felt I really hadn't wasted my time, after all."

Some art directors complain of having to see people who are emotionally disturbed or even abusive. Regrettably, that happens from time to time. Allowances must be made.

For the artist, there are many appropriate ways to ingratiate oneself to an art director; the best way is to exhibit good work and show restraint. Art directors, for their part, should make themselves as available as time permits. If it's not possible to devote office hours to this, then might I suggest attending portfolio reviews, such as those conducted at the School of Visual Arts, in which working professionals visit with students and critically view their work? Another method is classroom lectures, whereby students learn something about the process of art selection from the art director himself. Artists are grateful for the time, you may rest assured. But let the art director be forewarned not to be discouraged if most of the people he sees are not Rembrandts, El Lissitzkys, or Atgets. It is worth seeing them *all* simply to find the few with real talent. But more importantly, a service is being performed that is in the best interests of the entire field.

CREATING AN IDENTITY

A young illustrator's identity is more critical than that of a young designer, simply because the majority of illustrators will freelance, whereas the majority of designers will take on part-time or regular jobs. Moreover, illustration is decidedly more personalized and stylized than graphic design—at least in the beginning. Of course, for those young designers who have worked for a while and have decided to set up a freelance business or small firm, or for those courageous—or foolhardy—

enough to enter the business world right out of school, creating an identity is a major part of the process, too.

Since the requisites and methods for building an identity are somewhat different for the illustrator and designer, this section will address each separately. But, once again, please read the entire section: there are commonalities as well as differences, and the information for one may be applicable to the other.

THE ILLUSTRATOR This section presupposes that you are either working full time and freelancing on the side or that you are a full-time freelancer. In either case it is important to create some kind of presence—a niche for your work in whatever part of the marketplace you decide to enter. The possibilities are numerous and varied. For example, some illustrators work almost exclusively in the editorial area, others on book jackets, and still others will do virtually anything. Whatever your inclination, it is better for you to have a distinctive identity or trait rather than none at all.

In this case identity goes hand in hand with style, and style is many things. It is the identifiable surface manifestation of what you do as an artist— whether you are a realist, surrealist, or impressionist. Style also suggests media; for example, you might have a pen-and-ink or a watercolor style. Style indicates a manner—you might affect an art nouveau, art deco, or postmodern style. Finally, style is the context in which you create: you may choose an ornamental, conceptual, fantastical, or humorous style or employ them all. The English design critic Misha Black says that artists cannot work without at least stylistically reflecting the period in which they live.

In addition to having a recognizable style, an illustrator might also be identified with a specific genre, such as editorial, children's book, book jacket, medical, or technical illustration. Although it is better to be a generalist at the beginning than

29

Brad Holland, black-and-white cross-hatching.

Brad Holland, later style.

to limit oneself to a speciality, an effective portfolio, and hence a good identity, should ultimately highlight one's generic strengths.

If you limit yourself to one or two genres and a couple of styles, do not be afraid of being typecast at first. While it is sometimes difficult to experiment or otherwise change directions in the applied arts, it is nevertheless possible and even welcome. For years, Brad Holland was considered a black-and-white illustrator who cross-hatched, until he made a conscious effort to switch to color painting—and was accepted. Philippe Weisbecker made a radical departure from black-and-white cross-hatching to a more economical, delightfully abstract form that was greeted warmly by art directors. If your identity is true to your aesthetic and conceptual convictions, it cannot but change and grow over the years.

Reputation While an identity specifically relates to your work, a reputation is about you as a person—your ability to work well with others, deliver work on time, and solve problems. If you are consistently late, you will earn a bad reputation; if you cannot take direction, that will also be a point against you. Sometimes a so-called bad reputation does not prevent an artist from finding jobs; if your work is terrific, art directors can live with a temperamental artist. But, more often than not, the consistency with which you get assignments by one client, or are referred to others, depends on your reputation.

Naming Your Business It is not necessary for illustrators to come up with cute or pretentious titles. Your own name is sufficient, and art directors are more likely to remember the name Janet Doe than something like Dees and Does Studios. Furthermore, most art directors commission jobs from individuals, and some are put off by the idea of working with an organization. On the other hand, the studio title may give an art director the impression that an average illustrator has the strength of minions and that he or she does more than *just* illustration. Unless the beginner is going into business with others, however, he or she is better off using an unadorned, identifiable name.

Printed Matter   Although the illustrator need not go to the same trouble and expense as a designer to produce beautifully designed stationery, cards, bills, and promotions, it cannot hurt and might even enhance his or her identity. However, a beginning illustrator need only invest in a few essentials:

- ☐ letterhead and envelopes, which can be produced in a one-color, quick-copy job;
- ☐ mailing labels, which can be used instead of envelopes;
- ☐ a rubber stamp, which, if well designed, can be used instead of letterhead and envelopes—otherwise it should be applied to all artwork leaving the studio;
- ☐ billing forms, which can be photocopied or printed on letterhead; and
- ☐ reminder and promotion materials, as previously discussed.

Philippe Weisbecker, black-and-white cross-hatching.

At the beginning of your career, these items should be modest. As your client base grows, you will want to buy better printing and create more elaborate printed materials. However, even when the sky is the limit, try to keep things simple.

THE DESIGNER   If you accept full-time employment, little else is required to establish an identity. Use the time at the job to improve your portfolio and make contacts. Conversely, if you have decided to be a full- or part-time freelancer or to open a small business, creating an identity is a must.

Unlike the young illustrator, who must establish a style in addition to proving his or her skill, the young designer need only show an ability to do technically proficient and creative work. Such work

Philippe Weisbecker, later style.

need not be wed to (or mired in) any specific style or dogma; in fact, style is often a sign of rigidity rather than freedom. Your first clients are not going to be interested in how you can set the design world on its ear, but rather in how efficiently you can perform your task. If you do it with a modicum of competence and ingenuity, you will likely get more assignments. If you do enough assignments, you will become known to others.

Naming Your Business   Whether or not your name appears in the name of your business depends on two factors: ego and goals. The former is obvious; the latter involves long-term projections. These projections should take into account the possibility of future partners and expansion into other areas of design. In the beginning, though, the choice of a name is not critical—you can always change it.

The advice for illustrators applies to designers as well: if you are just starting to freelance, your name, alone, is appropriate. Titles do, however, imply a lot about your business practice, and in contrast to an illustrator, who works alone, a designer wants to give clients a sense of working with an organization. For example, *Mary Smith Design* suggests a studio of one, or a designer and an assistant. If you want to give the impression of a larger organization, try something like Mary Smith Design Associates or Bill Jones Design Office or The Janet Doe Organization. If you decide to team up with other designers, something like Mary Smith and Partners is possible (that is, of course, allowing for ego-free partners). Or try Smith and Jones, or Smith, Jones, Doe Design, if you want to convey a sense of staid professionalism. The possibilities are limitless.

Additionally, there is an infinite number of metaphorical, allusive, or just plain clever titles that pinpoint an essential characteristic of a business. Among the well-known ones are Pentagram (indi-

32

cating that the company originally had five partners), Push Pin Studios (the image of the push pin evoking the idea of commercial art or graphic design), Corp Com (a high-tech abbreviation for Corporate Communications), Whistlin Dixie (which evokes the studio's southern origins), and Manhattan Design (which conjures up the slick urbanity of New York City). However, beware of using this method to name your studio. Just because you have always wanted to call a business World Domination Design Studios, Bozo Design, Snail Studios, or Asylum Design, do not assume that a whimsical name is appropriate. Decide what kind of clientele you hope to address; whereas some clients enjoy a good joke, others may consider a clever or silly name unprofessional.

Unless you have multinational investors you will no doubt start out small and promote yourself as your assets and client base warrant. But as you grow, more business options will become available. You should know now the subtle classifications of business organization and how they are perceived by those in and out of the field:

☐ A *studio* suggests one or more people who work together. Usually, it services a small number of small to medium-sized clients. A studio may do all the things a firm does, but on a more limited basis. A designer working alone would never refer to him- or herself as a firm.

☐ A *firm* suggests a larger organization with one or more principals and the resources to serve a variety of clients in numerous ways—not only in graphic design, but in advertising, audiovisual, packaging, and so on. Design firms can have as few as three and as many as three hundred employees.

☐ An *office* straddles the fence between the preceding two classifications: it can be multifaceted, like a firm, or serve in a limited capacity, like a studio. *Office* is the right term for the lone designer who does not feel that *studio* accurately characterizes his or her business.

Printed Matter   All designers (freelance or not) should have at least a business card, and this should be tastefully designed to show typographic and color skills. But do not overdo it! If you are freelancing you must also have a letterhead and envelopes (do not be cheap in this regard). Well-designed mailing labels and billing forms enhance your overall print identity. The rest is determined by your need and desire to promote yourself.

Self-promotion for designers, as for illustrators, takes many forms. Buying into a _promotional annual_ is valuable only if you have something to sell. However, if you are a good letterer, logo designer, or chartmaker, this is a splendid way to have your work seen by agencies, studios, and firms. Most of the books are distributed gratis to art and design buyers around the country, and most will provide you with printed pages to send out to prospective clients or to leave as a reminder. Some designers buy space in periodicals that are not oriented specifically to graphic designers. For example, the California-based firm Vigon Seirrini advertises for fashion-conscious clients in _Interview_ magazine. _Sample folders_ or _booklets_ might include essentially the same material that can be found in a promotional page, but they usually show more examples, including real printed samples. Finally, _thematic posters, folders_, or _booklets_ can range from elaborate to simple. If the idea or concept is terrific, you can do it on a photocopy. If it is weak, no amount of fancy printing will help. The key is to show your conceptual savvy in the best possible light. Your materials should not be overly designed, but intelligently prepared to demonstrate your ability to wed idea, word, and image.

For illustrators and designers alike, selling oneself is an essential part of the applied arts business. Making the best possible impression on your clients, employer, and colleagues will earn you a reputation and ultimately contribute in creating an identity. Once you have decided upon a direction and a strategy, your portfolio is the most important tool in the selling process. And once you get work, your reputation will be determined by how well you live up to the promise of your portfolio and promotions.

3.
SETTING UP
SHOP

This chapter applies to all illustrators and designers who have chosen to freelance or to become otherwise self-employed. In addition to the various business options offered here, it is recommended that you consult an accountant before you set up any business, no matter how small.

Because this chapter is organized according to the size of your prospective business, beginning with a discussion of the least-ambitious freelance operation and continuing with the larger studio or office situation, a review of the semantic and physical differences between a studio, office, and firm is in order. Before deciding to set up shop, one should understand the following gradations. As defined by Dugald Stermer, illustrator, art director, and associate editor of *Communication Arts* magazine, in a *studio* everyone has a drawing table; in an *office* everyone has a drawing table except the principals; in a *firm* no one has a drawing table.

This humorous definition is actually a valid barometer of business progress. When starting out *you* will be handling almost all the work; a few years down the road you will begin to delegate certain responsibilities; and ultimately, you may reach a stage where you go beyond illustration and/or design into other realms of visual communication. Growth is a gradual process, with each step carefully planned. The best advice, therefore, is not to be too ambitious at the outset; take some chances if you must, but do not do anything until you feel it is right or necessary. Put even more succinctly:

- Start small
- Budget strictly
- Hire wisely

Although these words of advice may seem perfectly obvious, a surprising number of beginners ignore them, spending more than they earn and digging a financial hole from which it is difficult to escape.

Start small is an umbrella phrase for the whole process of setting up shop, and the maxim *do not overextend* is its corollary. Unless you are guaranteed regular billings or a consistent and reliable

36

client base (such as an illustration assignment each week for *Time* magazine or all the collateral promotion for IBM for one year), do not incur an unreasonable *nut* (your basic operating expenses). A client's fickleness may affect your financial picture; therefore, it is prudent to have more than one client before considering any upward movement. The various ways of starting small—working from home, sharing an office, or renting a small space—will be discussed in the following sections.

Budget strictly is usually anathema to the "creative" person. In fact, most artists find any thought of managing a business offputting. It is too bad that more art and design schools do not give mandatory courses in setting up shop, since the effectiveness with which one practices one's craft is directly proportional to one's income. How much you *have*, how much you *need*, and how much you *can spend* are very important determinants in renting space, paying taxes, producing promotions, making phone calls, and, yes, buying supplies. A strict budget will also determine how much you must charge for the work you are doing.

Hire wisely implies that you need assistance because you are busy. Do not hire unless absolutely necessary, because the minute you do, you will have incurred additional *overhead* (operating expenses that must be paid before you realize a profit). Keep in mind that if you need help, part-timers are always available, and students are always anxious to learn while they earn.

Given an understanding of these maxims, the following commonsense options for setting up shop will help you decide how much space you need and what supplies are sufficient to begin your practice. In addition to exercising your common sense, however, you should develop a *business plan*. This is usually a formal document that states your goals and aims for a given period (most often over the course of five years) and that projects your overhead, profit, fees, client base, and so on. You can work this out with an accountant or financial planner, which is advised, or you can do your own temporarily to test the waters. Perhaps within a year you will be ready for professional assistance.

BUSINESS SPACES

THE BEDROOM AND LIVING ROOM STUDIO

Unless you have already developed a clientele large enough to support the expense of an outside office, the most practical and economical place to start is out of your own home. Even some veterans, including Paul Rand and Brad Holland, continue to work in their homes, which have been equipped with all the necessary graphic arts tools and machines.

For the beginner, a modest investment in a drawing table, taboret, good lamp, comfortable chair, and small copier will transform any bedroom or living room into a temporary studio. However, since some might find living and working in the same rooms difficult or even depressing, those with more usable space should think about creating a room solely for work. Unless your living and working spaces are clearly defined, it will be difficult to entertain guests or conduct client meetings. Those with young children will find it essential to separate the family rooms from the working space to prevent jobs from being damaged. Whatever the arrangement, you must install a telephone and answering machine solely for work-related calls.

RENTING OFFICE SPACE A home studio can be made as efficient as an outside office, depending on your projected needs. For some, however, an office away from home is a psychological imperative.

The process of renting space is usually the same all over. Rents, of course, vary from locale to locale, but the formula for pricing is often consistent. Office rents are determined by the square footage of a space. Because what you pay for is not always usable, attempt to plan out the area before committing to it; you do not want to be stuck with less than you bargained for. Sometimes rents are discounted (or allowances given) based on the amount of renovation necessary. However, try not to involve yourself in that kind of negotiation until your business is on a firm footing. Remember that the space you rent today probably will not be adequate in half a year or more—you will need either a flexible or a short lease so that you will not be liable for excess rent if you decide to move. Of course, there are exceptions to this rule; if you find the perfect office at a great price, take it. Also remember that extra space may be sublet to bring in extra income. Many illustrators and designers help pay for their own spaces by renting portions to others in the profession.

Apart from size, improvement, and cost considerations, questions to ask yourself before renting include:

☐ Is the location appropriate to my needs? Will I be near an art supply store, stat house, type house, picture collection, restaurant, and so on?

☐ Is the neighborhood safe? Is the building secure?

☐ Can I and my clients gain access to the space twenty-four hours a day, seven days a week? Will a doorman or janitor remain on duty after business hours? Will the elevators continue to operate?

☐ Is there enough natural light? Will the space be warm enough in winter? Cool enough in summer?

☐ Are there kindred businesses in the same building?

SHARING SPACE Because there is economy as well as fellowship in numbers, many graphic designers and illustrators share offices or studios. Either they engage in the above-mentioned practice of subletting or they simply join forces with kindred souls to find a great space. Both options have the same advantages: the possibility of getting excellent space in a good locale for less money per person, and the company of other designers and illustrators, which takes the edge off of solitude. Moreover, with the right mix of people, more services can be provided to a larger client base. This type of relationship is purely for convenience, however, and is not to be confused with the collaboration involved in a studio or firm.

If you decide to share space, protect yourself at the outset from likely pitfalls:

☐ Make certain there is equal responsibility for the lease.

☐ Have a financial buffer, so that if one participant defaults the rest can afford to pay the rent.

☐ Plan your individual spaces before moving in. Make certain each of you is ensured optimum conditions from the start to avoid squabbles later.

☐ Create a reception area and meeting room, if possible.

☐ Allow for growth.

RENTING SPACE IN A STUDIO OR FIRM Many beginners and veterans find it advantageous to rent space from an existing studio or firm. Sometimes the space is a corner in the bullpen, other times it is a private office. The rents vary but are often negotiable depending on the services you can provide the host (for example, an illustration or design from time to time), or on the services the host can provide to you (for example, stats, type, and receptionist). Leases or agreements are often short-term, which means that you can leave whenever you choose (although it also means that you can be asked to leave whenever they wish).

For the beginner this situation is ideal: you can take advantage of the facilities and services, sometimes at a comparatively low fee; you are not isolated; and you are available for work if needed.

FURNISHING AND STOCKING YOUR STUDIO

When starting out do not commit yourself to expensive furniture or supplies. You will have no idea what is necessary until you have practiced a while.

Furniture for a home studio should be either compatible with your decor, or cheap and disposable if you plan to move to different quarters. In

either case you will need work surfaces, storage
and file cabinets, lighting, and so on. Any major
art supply store (A. I. Friedman, Arthur Brown,
and Charrette, among many others) will offer a
wide range of drawing boards, taborets, flat files,
lamps, and chairs, as well as scores of appliances,
such as paper cutters, pencil sharpeners, staplers,
tape dispensers, waxers, and more. Send for a
catalog.

Do not attempt to adapt your existing furniture to
the needs of graphic art. No matter how lovely your
antique rolltop desk may be, it does not provide
the right surface for drawing or doing mechanicals.
Regardless of how handsome that old oak swivel
chair may look, it will prove uncomfortable after
prolonged use. Comfort is an important health concern; beauty is not. The wrong chair will definitely
have long-term negative effects on your back or
other fragile parts of the body. In the short run, bad
furniture might cause restlessness.

The appliances you buy or rent (from pencil
sharpeners to copiers) should conform to your aesthetic needs, of course, but reliability and economy
are more important. Do not buy everything in matte
black, simply because it looks nice—you might
find that your tastes will change. Give yourself
some breathing room before committing to a specific aesthetic style. And keep in mind that you
may want to take some of these items with you to a
new space with an entirely different decor.

If you are renting an unfurnished office, you may
want to rent your furnishings as well. The beginner
will find that the start-up expense will be less than
the cost of buying what is needed (and will also
provide a better tax break, because one must de-
preciate purchases over the course of time, rather
than immediately deduct the monthly rentals). Office supply stores often rent furnishings and appliances. Shop around for the best deals on stat and
copier rentals and investigate buy/lease plans.

The young renter should also keep in mind that,
since the odds of moving a few times within the

course or a year are high, built-in shelves, drawers, and tables are unsound investments. Wait until you get a five- or ten-year lease before making that kind of commitment. And when you do, have built-ins constructed that can somehow be dismantled and preserved if you decide to move again.

Lighting and air-conditioning are extremely important for the renter (and everyone else for that matter). Spend the money for fluorescent lighting if good artificial light does not already exist, and have it installed by a professional. Moreover, unless you have a high tolerance to heat, an air-conditioner (the best you can get) is worth the money.

Keep yourself well stocked with whatever supplies are needed. Art supplies are expensive, so try to work out an arrangement with your local store or art supply dealer. Very often, customers with charge accounts who consistently order in quantity are given a modest discount.

For those sharing space, the above applies in spades. Sharing is tentative at best; you will not want to buy furniture as long as there is a chance that those with whom you are sharing will leave or default. Buy your own furniture, if you must, but rent as much common furniture and storage units as you can.

Those renting space in another's studio or office will usually be supplied with the essentials. You may, however, want to invest in a good chair, lamp, or even bookshelves, depending on the situation.

In all cases a separate phone and answering service is imperative. Do not share! The policing and bookkeeping woes are not worth the potential savings.

SERVICE NEEDS

Getting and furnishing your studio or office are only two aspects of setting up shop. You must also identify the services you will require and make the nec-

42

essary contacts with salespeople and vendors. These services are divided into intra-office and extra-office needs. The former might include maintenance of copy or stat machines, art supplies, and temporary help. The latter include stats and color prints; color comps and assemblies; typesetting; paper supply, postal, and messenger services; and printing.

The illustrator who does not design will have to be concerned with only a few of these requisites, such as art supplies, postal and messenger services, and perhaps temporary help, should he or she get a lot of work in the beginning. The illustrator/designer and the designer must be concerned with all.

Referrals from fellow professionals will be helpful in meeting intra-office needs; it is always best to copy what has been successful for the next person. Trial and error will determine extra-office needs. Designers are ultimately reliant on typesetting and printing services, which can be obtained through a referral, through an ad in the phone book, or through a listing in a supplier's guide. After doing business with a few typesetters and printers you will soon learn for yourself which are the best and worst in any given area. Here, however, are some hints that will help in making the right decisions:

Typesetting can be very expensive; shop around before settling on one or even two type shops.

Typesetting quality varies from company to company. In addition to a type specimen sheet or catalog, ask for sample settings to check on quality.

Some new type shops will gladly give you a discount to ensure your continued business. Although this is an accepted and mutually beneficial practice, get to know the capabilities of the shop before committing yourself implicitly to a long-term arrangement.

Different cuts of the same typeface range from excellent to terrible. Make certain that the typeshop has the cut you want.

Become aware of the new typesetting technologies.

An increasing number of typesetters accept personal computer disks or diskettes.

☐ Determine which printer is best for a particular job. Some do great posters yet falter on books. Some do multicolor work whereas others can handle only limited color. Some are always late whereas others can stick to a schedule.

☐ Learn about the various printing processes and techniques, including offset, gravure, thermofax embossing, and dyecutting.

☐ Learn from experienced professionals what to look for on a press check, so that your corrections are intelligent and intelligible. This will show your printer that you cannot be fooled by sloppy work.

☐ Build a respectful working relationship with all your vendors. You never know when you will need a favor.

TECHNOLOGY

Whoever sets up shop these days would find it difficult to ignore the effects of computer technology on contemporary graphic art. While many neophytes may not be in a financial position to buy machines that are capable of aiding design, and others may not be experienced enough to design on the screen, some basic understanding of the computer is necessary. For help in this area, keep abreast of the articles in computer graphics magazines and attend classes or seminars. Computer-aided design is not to be ignored. It is the future.

Beginning illustrators and designers should, moreover, save to buy a personal computer. For some, it will serve merely as an effective bookkeeping and word processing tool. Others will find that typesetting and chartmaking on computer will be more economical than through traditional means. There are many new design programs issued regularly, including those that can help you design type fonts, create photo-ready charts and graphs, and paginate newsletters and magazines.

44

Another significant tool for illustrators and designers is the Fax machine, which sends letter-perfect images over phone lines. This not only allows for the quick communication of rough, and even some finished, work from one part of the country to another, but it broadens the prospective client base considerably. With a printer attachment you will also be able to receive manuscripts and corrections over the phone line. The Fax is not cheap, but it is a good investment. Check with your electronics dealer for details.

Information about current technology is available from the computer and electronics outlets in your area. Learn about relevant equipment, and then price it carefully. Computers involve considerable investment, but if the system you select is appropriate, it will pay for itself in no time.

Once you have settled into your space, decided on a name, had your promotions, business cards, and letterhead printed, and organized your portfolio, you are about ready to practice. Before you do, however, ask fellow professionals about an accountant or lawyer (the best advice is to hire an accountant even for a short period each year). He or she will tell you about all the tax and legal obligations you will incur simply by opening your door for business, as well as about the benefits and pitfalls of loans and capital purchases. Although some of what you will hear is common sense, much more of it is acquired knowledge. Add to that the information offered in books, magazines, or seminars, and you should have the basics.

Setting up shop is as easy or as difficult as you make it. Do not be afraid to ask for help from fellow professionals or consultants, no matter how insignificant the problem may seem. People in this field are usually happy to give you the benefit of their experience. The following chapter on involvement in the design and illustration community will help you develop a network of support.

4.
MAKING
CONTACTS

Sometimes talent and skill are not the only ingredients of a successful career. As we have emphasized, selling yourself is as important as selling your work, and to this end you must make the right contacts with potential clients and employers. More important, friends and acquaintances within the field afford you a basis of support. Just as many jobs result from referrals by colleagues as from blind interviews—maybe more. A reputation built on the respect of others within the profession will go a long way toward opening the right doors all along the line. This chapter will discuss the various ways of making contacts, as well as the dos and do nots (the etiquette, if you will) of networking.

Regrettably, the term *networking* has its negative connotations. Coined in the seventies and applied to the venerable practice of social and business interaction, it has come to mean a process of self-promotion whereby one attends formal or informal social events primarily to make useful professional contacts. It follows that one contact will lead to others and that the process will be perpetuated to create a figurative web of supporters. In the eighties, networking has become so institutionalized and indicative of the age that it is the object of satire. Nevertheless, it is a necessary, and not all that painful, aspect of doing business which offers psychological as well as professional support, especially for lone and lonely freelancers.

MAKING CONTACTS WITHIN THE PROFESSION

Like all other professionals, practitioners of the graphic arts are members of a community of mutual concern. Regardless of their specialities, kindred spirits tend to come together out of united social, business, and educational interests. The varied means for establishing and maintaining the community include illustrators' and art directors' clubs, associations, societies, and institutes. Each has a particular agenda: Associations are usually trade or professional organizations that provide as much business guidance as social intercourse. Clubs and societies, such as the New York Art Directors Club and the Society of Illustrators, are often fraternal groups, offering a regular meeting place to socialize with colleagues and confer with clients. Institutes, such as the American Institute of Graphic Arts, are usually education- and advocacy-oriented.

All of these organizations exist in most states and large cities, depending, of course, on the number of graphic arts businesses in the region. The active ones organize conferences, seminars, and lectures and usually have regular meeting dates where dinner is served, ideas are shared, and special guests (often prominent members of the profession) talk about their work. Many groups are composed of both practitioners and suppliers, while others cater but are not restricted to specific disciplines. Examples of the latter include the Type Directors Club in New York and the Book Builders Association in Boston, both of which promote and encourage excellence in their respective fields, but should not be considered exclusive. Students and those just entering the field are encouraged to attend as many of the events sponsored by these groups as time and finances allow. This is the most effective way to meet new people and make contacts.

In addition to joining large organizations, designers and illustrators have recently begun to form smaller support groups that meet regularly to discuss creative and business issues, share news and information, and give advice when called for. In an article in the AIGA Journal, D. K. Holland encourages young and old designers to form such groups, pointing out that they are "good remedies for business inferiority. In the group context one realizes that business is not mysterious. One person is no dumber or smarter than the next guy. In a group there is combined knowledge valuable for all."

Whether you are an illustrator or a designer the process is the same. There are many ways to make yourself known to other professionals—peers and

seasoned veterans alike. Even the best-known designers and illustrators are accessible. However,
there is a right way and a wrong way to do it. There
is even an obnoxious way, which, like the relent-
less salesman, sometimes gets results, but is a
method that will not be touted here. The following
are some conventional yet effective approaches:

☐ Join an organization in your region that offers numerous programs (Part 3, Chapter 3 offers a list of
relevant associations, but please check into others
that may be located near you and that are especially suited to your interests).

☐ Do not be a passive member: go to meetings; introduce yourself to others; exchange telephone numbers; and show your work.

☐ Volunteer for committee jobs. Many organizations
retain a full-time, salaried director who relies on
members for organizing and overseeing programs
and events. Some organizations depend entirely on
members for administrative duties. Tasks include
inviting speakers; designing invitations and posters;
organizing membership drives; and scheduling
events. These are important responsibilities that
should not be taken lightly, and the duties, though
usually time-consuming, are direct links to the
community. With a good track record you might
eventually be elected an officer. Moreover you may
be able to propose unusual events that will enhance your reputation and organizational skills. If
you are a stranger in a new town, active involvement in an organization will speed up the process
of assimilation.

☐ Most organizations have annual competitions, and
many draw at least two-thirds of the jury from their
membership. Make it known that you would like to
be a part of the selection process. In addition to
valuable exposure to a body of other people's work,
you will meet and share insights with other jurors.

☐ Attend conferences, symposia, and lectures. Conferences, such as those sponsored by the American
Institute of Graphic Arts, the Society of Typo-

48

graphic Arts, the Poster Society, the Type Directors Club, and *American Illustration*, usually last for two or more days. The annual Stanford Design Conference at Stanford University and the Aspen Design Conference, sponsored by the Aspen Foundation, also offer the opportunity for more substantive contact with fellow professionals and others. Do not be afraid to introduce yourself to strangers; the people who attend these events want to meet new people. Business seminars (such as those conducted by the Design Management Institute) are equally valuable for the people seen and the information learned.

How much you can profit from any of the above situations is in part a result of how well you conduct yourself. The first rule (if one must call it a rule) is to take things in moderation. Do not appear too hungry, do not force yourself on anyone, and do not be transparent in your quest for fame and fortune. Other commonsense do nots of etiquette:

☐ Do not bring your portfolio to a social event and presume that someone will want to look at it. Art directors and studio managers resent being solicited for work at a social gathering. Rather, suggest to whomever you speak with that you would like him or her to see it at a convenient time; then call to make an appointment.

☐ Do not be a pest. Let people know that you are interested in having a conversation and follow up when the opportunity presents itself. Do not barge in on someone else's conversation and do not assume an air of close familiarity with a person you hardly know.

Social situations are difficult even for the seasoned veteran, so expect the occasional feeling that butterflies are attacking your stomach. Take a deep breath and try to follow some commonsense dos:

☐ Make an attempt to speak to new people. Introduce yourself and tell them a little about your work.

☐ If you sense some reciprocal interest, give that person your business card (not the big promotional flyer or folder you send to clients), or simply exchange telephone numbers.

☐ If you feel you have something to offer the group or organization whose event you are attending, seek out an officer and volunteer your services.

MAKING CONTACTS OUTSIDE THE PROFESSION

For the neophyte looking for a freelance or full-time position with a studio, firm, or publication, making contacts at a professional gathering is important. However, it is not the only way to get work. Because most potential clients never attend such functions, you must also rely on friends and acquaintances to expand your client base. It is difficult to predict how and when such opportunities will arise, but there are a few ways to make things happen:

☐ Join volunteer aid groups. For at least a decade socially concerned designers and illustrators have banded together to provide free or low-cost services for such causes as the nuclear weapons freeze, peace organizations, labor unions, political campaigns, agencies for the homeless, and anti-Apartheid groups. In addition to providing an invaluable service, it is an excellent way to meet colleagues and do some work of which you will be proud.

☐ On a decidedly more commercial note, scout the various goods produced in your locale for those that are poorly packaged. Very often a supplier or manufacturer has simply not thought seriously about enhancing his or her wares through graphic art. Make a pitch—all you have to lose is time, and if you are successful, you might land a profitable client or at least a good portfolio piece. Many small jobs will result in a thriving business.

☐ Finally, be sensitive to possible opportunities as they arise. If you hear about a new business venture, do not be afraid to ask if design or illustration is needed and do not be embarrassed to propose your services at the first opportunity. It is the only way to make your mark.

There is nothing wrong with getting to know people who can do you some good. Some day, when you are in a similar position, neophytes will be knocking on your door and you should be prepared to help them. Indeed, this is one way the field perpetuates itself. Just remember not to be overbearing, transparent, or manipulative. And remember too that your work will ultimately speak loudest and most effectively. It is recommended that, whatever your field, you apply for membership in the American Institute of Graphic Arts (a national group with local chapters). At least one additional membership in a local concern will be advantageous. For an annotated list of the most active professional clubs and associations in the United States and Canada, see Part 3, Chapter 3.

5.
GETTING DOWN TO BUSINESS

Now that you have a basic introduction to the options and an understanding of the means to get a foothold in the applied arts, now that you have read the encouraging advice and the cautionary notes, it is time to learn a little about business—all those financial and legal dos and do nots that they rarely, if ever, teach you in school. One practitioner poetically calls this the "dark side of his creative moon," however, the business end can be challenging, if not creative. Leslie Smolan, a principal of the New York-based design firm Carbone Smolan Associates, confided in an article in the *AIGA Journal* that "business never bores me. It's conceptual. It may turn out to be numbers on a piece of paper, but it still involves looking at a complete picture and knowing what it means." Knowledge of business basics will keep you from being a wage slave and help you to become solvent and successful. A complete treatment of this subject would require a book in itself, and there are, in fact, a number of excellent books that we encourage you to read carefully:

The Business of Graphic Design, by Ed Gold (Watson Guptill)
From a review by Roger Whitehouse in the *AIGA Journal*: "Instructive and covers every potential issue that designers must confront in running their own businesses. Although the book deals with the most elementary steps, it also gives considerable insight and practical advice on many more sophisticated issues, such as chapters on scheduling, including milestone charts, bar charts and critical path flowcharts."

Graphic Artists Guild Handbook: Pricing and Ethical Guidelines, compiled by D. K. Holland (Graphic Artists Guild)
Necessary reading for all freelancers and small-studio principals. Offers intelligently detailed listings of all manner of business practices, from contracts to copyright protection.

*Selling Your Graphic Design and Illustration: The
Complete Marketing, Business and Legal Guide*, by
Tad Crawford and Arie Kopelman (St. Martins)
A how-to guide for the graphic arts, covering marketing, business, and law. Also discussed are
methods for increasing visibility and identity. Includes many lists of potential markets, income
ranges, and growth areas.

*Legal Guide for the Visual Artist: The Professional's
Handbook*, by Tad Crawford (Madison Square)
The author, a lawyer specializing in the graphic
arts, has succinctly identified potential problem
areas for designers and illustrators, with respect to
taxes, billing, insurance, and so on.

As an adjunct to these invaluable handbooks, this
chapter will review several commonsense business
practices and will indicate areas to be explored before and after you have set up your shop. Although
some of the topics have been touched on in Chapters 2 and 3, they are definitely worth repeating.

DEVISING A BUSINESS PLAN

Before setting up shop in your home or office,
alone or with partners, you must ask yourself some
basic questions and supply some definite answers:
- What do I need to earn?
- What do I want to earn?
- What type of work do I want to do?
- How will I go about getting this work?
- On what shall I base my fees?
- How much shall I charge?

If you cannot answer these questions, stay at
your job—you are not ready to start your own business. If you are really serious, you will not just
pose and answer these questions informally but will
engage a financial adviser to help you organize a *financial plan* and a *growth projection*.
In its simplest form the financial plan is a docu-

ment indicating how much you will need to cover expenses—what is required to pay the rent, utilities, suppliers, and employees. It will give you an idea of how much you can expect to earn in fees over a given period. By mapping out your cash-flow versus your income, it will also contrast the amount of profit you may hope to make with a more realistic picture of your potential earnings.

The growth projection is a similar document that details your five-year plan, including office space, promotion, staff, and equipment requirements versus estimated income. Although you can create these documents yourself, it is more efficient to prepare them with a financial consultant.

Success is ultimately measured by growth, but keep in mind that *growth* is a relative term. Your business should expand both according to your willingness to grow and the speed with which you can reasonably do so. Megaprofits are not the only measures of success. A reasonable plan or projection will take into account your personality. If you choose to wade before you swim, that is perfectly all right. It may take years before you will feel comfortable making money, and some people are never comfortable doing it. Remember, however, that just as one's creativity can be assessed by adventurous exploration and personal growth, one's business abilities likewise depend on an understanding that the marketplace is dynamic. Even if you only grow to meet the rising cost of living, some expansion of your financial boundaries is necessary, indeed, inevitable.

Some practitioners begin very small; then as their confidence and expertise grow, so do their businesses. An illustrator may take on assistants, or a designer may hire an associate or extra staff to help with mechanicals. Working space may be enlarged to meet the needs of an expanding client base. If this has been predicted in a plan, you will probably have the means to accomplish growth with little trauma. If it comes suddenly, as, for example, when a big client unexpectedly appears on the scene, then a new plan will probably be necessary.

Although one often feels tempted to think big, it is best to start small and take cautious steps. You must deal with several rudimentary areas before business can be conducted, including, registering your business with the local government department, setting up a bookkeeping and records system, getting information about insurance and taxes, and establishing credit with suppliers and the bank.

When first starting out, people often have the sense (or lack of sense) that these mundane matters do not affect them. One young neophyte said, "I have plenty of time before I have to do *real* business stuff." Well, if by "real business stuff" he meant paying taxes or keeping records, he should wait until the first quarterly tax bill or Internal Revenue audit comes around. Those eventualities are more terrifying than entering the "adult" world of business. It is never too early to practice properly. But remember too that getting off on the wrong foot is not necessarily a long-term tragedy— you have a lifetime to do it right.

DEVELOPING FEES AND LEARNING ABOUT COSTS

One of the most valuable pieces of general advice for the beginner is: *Never spend more than you make.* This means, simply, do not budget a job in excess of what you can afford to spend in doing it (unless you can sustain the loss temporarily). Know your overhead costs and develop a fee structure (either a flat fee or hourly rate) based on what you need to meet those costs. The Graphic Artists Guild and various management seminars offer excellent advice in these matters, but a few guidelines are provided here. Generally your fees should be based on:

overhead, which includes rent, electricity, supplies, telephone and hired help;

■ *expenses,* which include all out-of-pocket job expenditures, such as type, stats, c-prints, and so on; and

■ *profit,* or what you would like to net based on your monthly estimate or yearly projections.

You should always build a buffer somewhere into your calculations to account for extensive corrections, client indecision, printing rate increases, illness, or any other unexpected development. The worst situation is to finish a tough job and realize that you have nothing to show for it.

Requesting payment is one of the most difficult things a beginner can do. Am I worth it? Should I really be paid for this? are questions commonly asked even by some veterans. "Artists should not have to ask for money," is another bizarre canard. Remember, however, that you have expenses to meet and need food to eat, and that the client is in a position to pay for your services. If you have trouble telling the client what you want, give him or her a formal estimate written on your stationery (this should be done whether you speak to the client or not, so that you have a record). Also ask for a certain percentage up front. If possible, make allowances for any additional work the client may want in excess of the original estimate.

CONDUCTING BUSINESS THE RIGHT WAY

Assuming you have produced promotions, advertised in the annuals, made the rounds, given your estimates, and acquired your first clients, the work has only just begun. Nine times out of ten, getting the job is easier than doing it. Graphic design and illustration, after all, require both creativity and execution. And although creativity takes time and effort, execution demands twice as much. When starting out, do everything possible to ensure that your work will look good. An illustrator should know his or her media fluently; in other words, he or she must recognize what will and will not print in any environment. A designer must have a command of all the processes and, even more than an illustrator, must be a good *production manager*. If your printer is inferior, the best idea will become the worst junk. It is your responsibility to follow through at every stage. Go to the press checks. If you are not doing the mechanicals yourself, watch over them—and *sign off* on everything. If this means hiring a part-time assistant, budget that into your expense projection.

Illustrators must spend whatever time it takes to understand the assignment. If you have a representative, do not take the easy way out by letting him or her pick up and deliver your work. Any questions should be discussed directly with the client. Learn about the approval process. How many sketches must you show and to whom? Is there a kill-fee in the event the sketches are not approved? Deliver the job yourself so that if the worst happens and any changes must be made, you will hear about them firsthand. Show that you care about the job regardless of its size. Remember, small jobs often lead to big ones if the client is happy. Moreover, in a direct relationship you are in a position to explain yourself, if necessary. Fear and shyness are not adequate reasons for avoiding contact with your client. Lack of time is the only viable excuse, and time should be budgeted from the outset to avoid conflict.

The designer is in a slightly different position. Unlike the illustrator, who usually does only one part of a larger project, the designer often manages a complete entity. Keep the word *managing* in mind. Ultimately, as a principal in a design studio, you will be managing an account and administering to the needs of your client, and most clients hate being ignored or put on a back burner. A good analogue of the bad graphic design manager is the building contractor who, having taken on many jobs to make a living, has only a modicum of time to spend with each client and is besieged by phone calls from the frustrated and angry folks he is not attending to. This scenario is a fact of life in the contracting business (at least when the economy is good) but it need not be the case in the design business. Moreover, if one is not happy with the performance of a contractor, it is difficult to get someone else (it seems that every contractor practices the same folly to a greater or lesser extent), whereas so many designers are graduated each year that the client can revel in a buyer's market. If your performance is unreliable, you can be replaced.

To avoid this situation, designers and illustrators alike must schedule their time for maximum efficiency. One simple rule of business practice is to maintain an efficient datebook, calendar, or scheduling system. They can range in scale from a simple desk reference that shows your daily projects at a glance to a large weekly or monthly bulletin board that allows you and your colleagues quick access. A pocket- or briefcase-size calendar is also worthwhile. Other time-management tools, such as products like File-A-Fact and Time Saver, are available at any well-stocked stationery store. These are desk and briefcase diaries used to record appointment times, notes from meetings, and long- and short-term plans.

If you are more ambitious and have a penchant for organization, you should also create job sheets that show not only the time that has been allotted to a specific project, but how long you estimate the project to take. Ultimately, they will help you with current billings and (because they are accurate records of time expended) with determining how much to charge in the future.

You might find that your schedule will be tight at a specific time of year. For example, design firms dealing with corporate annual reports usually become exceptionally busy in January, February, and March because of changes, press okays, and so on. Book jacket designers, on the other hand, feel the crunch during late fall and spring because most publishing houses have two selling seasons. At those times it is prudent to bring in extra help—a mechanical artist, an expediter, or even someone to answer the phone. When you are just starting to get work, nothing should be spared that helps you to meet your deadlines.

BUSINESS ETHICS

Although one can easily *say* that nothing should be spared in terms of your time and money, the reality of the situation is, of course, that neither resource is inexhaustible. Nevertheless, corners should not be cut and questionable business procedures should not be practiced. In addition to having creative and technical abilities, illustrators and designers must have ethical sensitivity. This comes in many forms:

☐ personal ethics (that is, jobs one should or should not take for political or moral reasons);

☐ business-to-business ethics (do not cheat on financial obligations to suppliers or employees);

☐ business-to-client ethics (do not overcharge or welch on a deadline);

☐ creative ethics (do not steal another's ideas).

These are commonsense tenets; however, in the heat of business, as in the heat of battle, one is sometimes quick to abandon the civilities.

Practitioners should also be aware that an ethical code is not a one-way street. There must be a *quid pro quo* or the system will not work. If you are being deceived by a client or a supplier, there is recourse. The books listed at the beginning of this chapter focus on potential danger areas and offer guidelines for coping with them in a professional manner. The options include redressing grievances through joint ethics committees (which are usually local panels empowered to act on practitioners' complaints against employers and contractors), or presenting them before small claims court or higher judicial bodies. Most important, the books provide lessons in contractual obligation (for example, what protections are offered and what problems to avoid in a contract), which is as much a safeguard for you as it is for the client. Read those sections carefully.

Being a responsible business person involves being responsible to yourself as well as to your suppliers and clients. You can protect your endeavor from the outset by creating a business plan, deciding on reasonable fees, and establishing an environment in which to do good work.

Illustration and design most definitely can be taught, but a formal artistic education is not always necessary. Many successful practitioners, Brad Holland and Rudolph de Harak, for example, never took a drawing, layout, or typography course, having decided instead to learn from experience. Some designers, such as Tibor Kalman, simply stumbled into the field; when forced to produce that first printed piece, they acquired the hands-on knowledge necessary to make it work.

Often you can get the most valuable educational experience in a printing plant, type shop, or photo lab, simply by asking questions while waiting for a job to be completed. In the classroom of the streets there is no time for the theoretical; instead, commonplace techniques, which to the uneducated are mysterious technical processes, are acquired by observing, and in some cases doing, jobs that most designers and illustrators allow others to do. Even if you never again have to assemble a job photographically or set your own type, the firsthand experience gives you insight into the technical possibilities that will ultimately contribute to design proficiency. This statement, however, is not intended to devalue formal, even theoretical, education. Intensive course work in aesthetic and technical areas is the most effective way to learn the basics and develop a working vocabulary. Without an understanding of the fundamentals of drawing, typography, color, and spatial relationships, intelligent practice is at best limited and at worst impossible.

CONTINUING EDUCATION

Although some practitioners are resolutely self-taught, most get certificates or degrees from various arts schools or universities after completing a three- to four-year academic or work/study program. Depending on the quality of the teachers in a given institution, this sort of education usually more than suffices to propel graduates into entry-level jobs.

6. CONTINUING EDUCATION AND TEACHING

Sometimes, though, further education is necessary either to round out one's general knowledge or to impart information about a specialized area. For example, an artist who wants to practice animation must take a few film and animation courses before plying the craft; a production assistant who wants to be a designer might take courses in basic or advanced typography; an illustrator who is doing decorative or technical work could take a course in "conceptual" illustration to broaden his or her markets; and an art director interested in the new technologies might take a computer graphics course. For those who are interested in teaching, continuing education courses are given on the history of graphic art.

Do not be concerned that class attendance may conflict with your work schedule. Literally hundreds of career enhancement courses are offered at night, during the summer, or on weekends. These range in subject from rudimentary mechanical instruction to life drawing to artistic theory. Milton Glaser's design and illustration tutorial, offered by the School of Visual Arts in New York City, is the most well known, attracting people from all over the world—professionals and students alike—for an intensive semester of workshop projects. If you are interested in taking such courses, check out the art school in your area or write for catalogs from institutions in other parts of the country.

WORKSHOPS AND SEMINARS In addition to regularly scheduled courses in colleges and art schools, some graphic arts organizations, as well as some individuals, offer limited workshops in virtually all areas of interest. For many years the American Institute of Graphic Arts has offered "clinics" for the analysis of specific design problems. Similar programs are now given by AIGA chapters. The Society of Newspaper Designers sponsors a week-long workshop in "newspaper graphics" (illustrated charts and graphs), which attracts both seasoned and young professionals. Every year the Illustrators' Workshop runs a two-week program in some exotic locale. Featuring lectures and labs by many well-known professionals, this event affords beginners the opportunity to make contacts and create portfolio pieces. Other regular and occasional workshops are listed in Part 3, Chapter 3.

GRADUATE PROGRAMS Some practitioners—young and old alike—recognize the need for a long-term postgraduate education. Different motives govern people's decisions: the untrained aspirant to a graphic arts career enrolls to gain the knowledge necessary to launch him or her in a new profession; the seasoned professional looks to expand his or her conceptual and technical skills; the neophyte may be drawn by the opportunity to acquire contacts; and the graduating art student is perhaps postponing (out of fear of unpreparedness) the time when he or she must enter the work world. For some, a graduate degree offers a certain cache. It is in keeping with social trends and values which dictate that a higher education is the *sina qua non* of a true professional. For others, postgraduate study bestows knowledge and proficiency that undergraduate study or even a job cannot provide, because it intensely exposes the student to very specialized work. Some postgraduate programs offer invaluable exposure to masters in the field (such is the case with Paul Rand at Yale). And for those who want to teach on a permanent basis, the M.F.A. is a passport into the academic world.

As we have stressed, making contacts is one of the key aspects of building your career, and school—whether a graduate or continuing education program—will give you access to people who can be helpful. Teachers often recruit assistants and freelancers from among their students—after all, the student learns everything that would have been learned by an assistant hired through an advertisement or recommendation. If you decide to continue your education, it is important to choose classes that are taught by teachers with whom you would like to work and, once enrolled, to do your best stuff. The odds are that you will be noticed. Since designers and art directors are always looking for entry-level personnel, and since some illustrators benefit greatly from an assistant, you are in an excellent position to be hired or at least recommended to others.

Additionally, school is fertile ground for building professional relationships with peers. One learns how to collaborate and share insights. Indeed, some well-known affiliations, such as Push Pin Studios, began with the merger of like-minded students and grew into full-fledged businesses.

Finally, the graduate school experience is helpful for developing ancillary employment. A good student is often seen as a potentially good teacher, and teaching can be another career building block.

Although the contacts made in school are important, keep in mind that an illustrator or designer neither will be offered nor refused a job on the basis of his or her educational background. A degree or certificate is not the determining factor. The work is what counts. Although it helps to be articulate, knowledgeable, and self-assured, and education is a means to develop those traits, it is only one means. Given the right graduate program and exposure to an astute instructor, however, one's sphere of understanding will increase in ways that cannot but help a career.

Art schools, colleges, and universities throughout the country are establishing more and more M.F.A. programs in design and, less frequently, illustration. The most prestigious schools, including Cranbrook Academy, Yale University, and the Art Institute of Chicago, are now vying with other institutions for students because better programs are being created in once backwater schools.

If you have decided to apply to a graduate program, it is prudent to ask yourself exactly what you want out of an education and to investigate the options carefully. For example, Cranbrook differs significantly from Yale in several ways. First there is the question of faculty. Yale has significant modern masters, including Rand, Bradbury Thompson, and Alvin Eisenman, plus guest lecturers. Cranbrook has a basically younger, perhaps less renowned, group. More important, the two schools differ in terms of approach: Cranbrook is known for its theoretical orientation, specifically in the realm of design "deconstruction" (sometimes referred to as *new wave*), and for its emphasis on furniture, fabric, interior, and architectural design. Yale is known for its Bauhaus and Swiss affinities.

In the realm of illustration, Syracuse University's part-time graduate program, which emphasizes extracurricular work/study projects differs significantly from the M.F.A./Illustration program at the School of Visual Arts in New York City, an intensive two-year course that stresses classroom instruction and student interaction. Some programs discourage a "school style," whereas others encourage students to work and think similarly. Some stress outside, hands-on experience, whereas others keep education confined to the campus. Before the admissions director questions you, you should determine your own needs and interests.

Part 3, Chapter 4 lists some of the art schools, colleges, and universities that offer graduate degrees in design and illustration. Write for the catalogs and explore the programs carefully before committing yourself to the time and expense of extra schooling.

TEACHING FULL OR PART TIME

There are two kinds of design and illustration teachers, the full-time teacher or professor and the part-time instructor. The former can be (and often is) a practitioner in a limited way, whereas the latter is primarily a practitioner who teaches his or her specialty on the side. While full-time teaching is very valuable and certainly rewarding, most de-

65

signers and illustrators who have a penchant for pedagogy choose the part-time route. The faculties of many art schools are made up of part-time professional instructors, and some colleges and universities employ a certain percentage of adjunct or visiting instructors, who teach for a limited period.

For the young professional, part-time teaching can be a valuable experience. Simply taking on the responsibility of sharing knowledge with others is a major step in the process of becoming a seasoned practitioner. The assignments and subsequent critiques given to students can be equally informative for the teacher.

Although someone just out of school is not always the best candidate for a teaching job, recent graduates sometimes have the clearest ideas of what students need to know. Do not be afraid to suggest a new course to the chairperson of an art school or college; you may have an idea that will round out the curriculum.

Many young designers and illustrators, believing that they have something special to impart, teach night or day school courses. Art school and college catalogs are replete with such commonplace course titles as Introductory Mechanicals, Learning to Spec Type, Advertising Comps, and Storyboard Rendering, as well as other, intriguing titles, such as Drawing from the Guts, Making Type Speak, Book Proposals and Packaging, Designing for the Public Sector, and so on. Most department chairpersons are open to new course ideas, and many are willing to include the description in the catalog to see how many students apply.

Continuing education is imperative for those interested in changing careers to the applied arts, and it may be a valuable experience for those who are already established in the field. The best advice is to judge for yourself what more you would like to accomplish, what your speciality should be, what skills must be honed, and whether or not a job, a night school course, or a graduate school program is the best way to enhance your professional status. If you opt for further education, then select your courses or program carefully. Decide whether or not you must work as well as attend classes and, if so, for how long. There are many interesting possibilities; do not merely settle for the most expedient.

CASE HISTORIES
–WORDS FROM
THE WISE

PART
TWO

The following interviewees represent professionals involved in a broad range of the applied graphic arts—graphic designers who work in large, medium-size, and small studios; illustrators; teachers; artists' representatives; and even a business therapist. The information is valuable enough, and the length of each interview short enough, to warrant a complete reading of this section regardless of your specific area of interest.

MARSHALL ARISMAN is a freelance illustrator whose work appears regularly in many national publications. He is also cochairman of the media arts department and chairman of the M.F.A./Illustration program at the School of Visual Arts in New York City.

As the head of a major illustration department and an illustrator yourself, what do you think is the best way to prepare a portfolio for viewing by the outside world?

There are two common approaches to portfolios. Some instructors feel the portfolio should be eight to ten pieces, that it should include a wide variety of subject matter—everything from a product design to an editorial piece. The other point of view is that there shouldn't be anything in the portfolio that you don't feel strongly about. The truth is that the two portfolios get you different kinds of work. I mean, if you go out with a generalized portfolio, you tend to get hired for your skills rather than for your conceptual ability. If you go out with work that you feel strongly about in terms of content, you tend to get hired for that kind of job. It seems practical to do a more diversified portfolio, but in the long run you do better by going out with work that actually means something to you. A generalized portfolio may get you work faster, but in the long haul it is not very distinctive. That's the dilemma in freelancing; and there is no real wisdom about where to start.

70

Do you think that the portfolio will make the ultimate difference?

The minute you leave school and decide to freelance, you are in the same market, competing for the same page in *Esquire* or any other publication, along with everyone else—veterans and students. The casualty rate is very high. From watching students over the years, I've learned that it's not even a question of talent; it's a question of what personal qualities keep someone out there making telephone calls and seeing people over a four- to five-month period. For freelancers, the ability to make telephone calls is at times probably as important as talent.

Given that the perservering freelancer has made it past the secretary and has an appointment, what level of creative or stylistic development would be necessary for him or her to be confident about getting the job?

Well, you can't enter this market without what an art director perceives as a style. In other words, you can't go out there with a little of everything, without a direction. You have to be formed enough so that the work shows a level of consistency. This will convince the art director that he or she is going to get something acceptable back.

Should the portfolio have a particular format to communicate this direction most effectively?

I don't think so. Everyone has played the endless game of rearranging the portfolio. It is probably good therapy, but I don't really think it matters.

I would always rather see originals, but that is a personal bias. I think it is a matter of simply presenting the work cleanly. I don't think a matte or lamination ever gets you the job. It's a little different if you are a designer. Your portfolio becomes part of your design presentation. But for an illustrator, I think it is a question of just protecting the work.

Do you offer frank critiques of portfolios? If so, on what do you generally comment?

I'm very honest because it really doesn't help anyone if I don't tell the truth. But truth is relative, and opinions will vary. The advantage of showing the portfolio to a number of people is that you get a wide variety of opinions. Then you can make your own decisions.

Do you encourage illustrators to practice graphic design?

No. We used to require a great deal of design in the illustration curriculum. What happened was, we turned out people who were half-baked illustrators and half-baked designers. At the School of Visual Arts the illustration major is a pure major. There are classes available to do graphics, but they are not requirements. Again, this is personal. I think it is the art director's job to do the layout, not the illustrator's.

In the nearly twenty years that you have taught, many successful and unsuccessful artists have passed through. Are there any general signs that indicate the potential success or failure of a student?

Well, unfortunately, students that have very tight and rendered work tend to get jobs faster. But the casualty rate in illustration is enormous; it's just the nature of the beast. The economics of living in the city are very tough, and in order to freelance you have to live in a large city. That makes it a career that one must really want very badly, and you have to be lucky enough to find some means of support until you begin getting work regularly.

What, if anything, is the right mental and physical attitude for going out on an interview?

Whether you wear a suit or dress casually hardly matters at all. Art directors are like anyone else; they want to work with people who are highly motivated, interested, and excited by what they do. If you are lethargic about your work, you're probably going to lose out to someone who is committed and energized. Remember, you can't talk an art director into liking your work or impress him with neatness or politeness. My advice is to keep your mouth shut and let the art director look. If he or she likes it there's no need to sell it.

Even though you are the chairman of the M.F.A./Illustration program, do you honestly believe that graduate school really is necessary for the average illustrator?

There are very few M.F.A. illustration courses— only three in the entire country. There are probably good reasons for that. One is that most students who get to the end of their four-year undergraduate school are burning to get out there and see what happens to them. They are different from fine arts students, who basically think: "Well, now I have to go to graduate school because some day I'll teach." I don't think most illustrators think about teaching as a career. The only justification for SVA's illustration graduate program is that it really isn't about extending your undergraduate portfolio so much as it's about trying to learn to write and to make pictures that result in a unique and inclusive package. The point of the program is to draw on subject matter from real-life experience. In essence, it's about trying to give some power back to the illustrator.

You mentioned the travails of the big city before. What else is problematic for the newcomer entering the big city—specifically New York?

The basic problem is that people tend to think of the city in terms of, "I'll come to New York and I'll give myself a month to see if I can make it." It doesn't work that way. All that's going to happen in a month, unless you're very lucky and get a job immediately—which is rare—is that you will begin the process of breaking new ground. It is actually quite simple. If someone really likes your portfolio, they'll refer you to somebody else, and it just goes on and on. If you're any good, you'll continue to work through this introductory period, so that by the end of three months, you'll probably have thrown three pieces out of your portfolio and added three new pieces. Then you'll have to start all over again and see the people that you saw two months before. So, my advice is to find some way to mentally give yourself at least six months.

The other problem is simply trying to protect yourself from being paranoid. That is the freelance dilemma. A lot of art directors won't see illustrators and prefer drop-offs. What tends to kill people is the anonymous process. You drop off the portfolio and you pick it up the next day. There is no note inside, no comment at all. You don't know if anyone actually looked at it, and that's tough.

As I said before, you must really want this badly, because you're going to pay a lot of dues. But actually I *like* the process. It is quite direct, and I think that most of the time art directors usually do make the right choices. It is a straightforward business. There is no graft that I'm aware of; there's not enough money for there to be graft. I've never heard of an illustrator paying off an art director. It really does come down to the quality of your work. Illustration is a process of wanting to develop your art as it relates to the printed page. That's quite exciting and, if it works, a great deal of fun.

MICHAEL ARON is the principal of Michael Aron Graphic Design, which he started alone after working three years for Herb Lubalin and then another three years for Pushpin Lubalin Peckolick.

What is the major difference between working for someone else and working for yourself?

There's more freedom, of course, in working for myself. But even as an employee I was very lucky. When I worked for Seymour Chwast and Herb Lubalin I was given a lot of creative freedom and I had quite a few of my own clients. But although they allowed me to have fun, I still worked in a manner designed to please them. So, ultimately, it's more fun to be on my own and to do it completely my own way.

When starting out, working for someone is really the best thing to do. For a student just out of school it is a good way to accumulate experience. The mistakes one makes are at someone else's expense, so to speak.

Moreover, you can learn invaluable lessons about suppliers because, after all, half of the design process is about dealing with suppliers—printers, typesetters, binders, et cetera—and getting the work produced. What you are promised and what you get from a supplier is going to make you look either good or bad in the client's eyes. If the printing doesn't get delivered in time, or if it's badly done, you are in great jeopardy of losing the client. It's very difficult to know who the good suppliers are when you're just out of school. A staff job allows you to get to know them, and they get to know you, so that when you start your own business they'll service you as well as they did before.

After so many years of being an employee, setting up your own place must have been frightening. What did you do to make the switch easier?

The most important thing before starting a studio is to have clients in the wings. The practical aspects, like getting space and buying furniture, are easy, but if you don't have the work, then it's all uphill. The reason I started was because I knew that I had a list of committed clients.

You seem to have approached this cautiously. What about other practicalities and protections, such as hiring a lawyer or an accountant?

I'm a good example of someone who is doing this on a small, manageable scale. It's just me and an assistant. I didn't need to incorporate; I didn't need a lawyer. I need an accountant, but that's only two or three times a year. I believe that if one has a feeling for business, then it can be handled personally.

Cash flow is the most important issue when starting out. You have to be willing to spend some of your own money or get a loan. With the first couple of small jobs, I had to cover the printing and the typesetting expenses, and sometimes those costs were high. In fact, I needed between $10,000 and $20,000 to get started on a small scale. I know other designers who have started studios on a much bigger scale, aiming at the $100,000 accounts. That's a different game. I am interested in billing jobs between $2,000 and $10,000, plus expenses.

In addition to having a bit of a cushion, one accepted way to cover yourself is to ask for an advance against the job—around one-third up front is the standard rate. But I found that in my first year of business it was hard to get the money because it was hard for me to ask for it. It was a political decision on my part to spend my own money. Fortunately, I wasn't burned.

Planning ahead is also very important. Just because you might be busy one week doesn't mean there will be work the next. Scheduling clients for the weeks and months ahead is necessary, because the worst thing that can happen is that you finish a project and there is nothing in the wings to start on.

You could have started more modestly by setting up shop in your home. Why did you choose to begin your business in an outside office?

It's very important to have an office that is separate from home, so that when clients come by they feel like they're dealing with a reliable business. And the office has to be in a nice neighborhood. If you're working in a city like New York, there are a lot of areas that are not conducive to professional business. But there is also plenty of small office space around that's still affordable.

Although it's not what I prefer, one can also share studio space. In New York, specifically, there are many ads in the *Village Voice* and in the classified section of the Graphic Artists Guild newsletter that say "Graphic designer wanted to share studio." There seems to be growth in the area of shared arrangements, where someone might take an entire floor in a building and split it up.

Once you were set up, did you do any self-promotion to broaden your client base?

My promotion is actually tied in with moving, because the event is a good excuse to send everyone an announcement. But number one on the list of self-promotions is to enter all the juried shows and competitions. Acceptance puts you in a select group that invariably gets positive attention.

I don't feel that a designer working on a small scale has to do an elaborate, general self-promotion. If you want to work for client X, then you have to go after that one individual or company with a series of mailings, letters, and meetings. General promotions won't help much.

You said that you take on only moderately budgeted accounts. Are there jobs you would not do?

One should be very selective about the type of work accepted, because whatever you start doing can and will be perpetuated. If you do a certain kind of job, then the odds are high that you're going to do another job like it afterwards. You want to make sure that the jobs you do are the things you'll be comfortable with. Turn down the work that you don't want to do. Don't do it just for the money.

The next stage, once the work begins to come in, is creating an economic structure. What do you do about billing and cash flow?

I use a system of three-time markup, which is figured based on an hourly rate. I decided, for example, that I need to earn $20 clear for time spent on any job. I then multiply that sum by three when I bill the client. So, it's $20 for my labor, $20 to cover overhead, which includes the rent, lights, art supplies, et cetera, and finally $20 for profit. That equals a rate of $60 per hour. Expenses are always billed additionally.

What about taxes? Is that not a danger area?

It means I have to be aware that between 35 and 40 percent of what I earn belongs to the government. This must be paid on a quarterly basis, so I have to save—have a reasonable cushion in the bank—and be conscious that every three months I need a certain amount of cash. The accountant is important here because he will determine how much is necessary.

A small design studio is actually very easy to run, compared to other businesses. It's pretty straightforward. You do a sketch or a finish, you send a bill, you get a check. There is no tremendous amount of paperwork; one just has to keep track of receipts—which is not difficult, even for the disorganized person.

How do you keep order?

I have "job bags," a numbered envelope for each job; and everything that relates to that job goes into the envelope.

It is also important to put everything in writing. Every time you quote a price, send out a letter confirming it and have it signed by the client and returned, so that no problems arise later. These signed letters do not have to be long or elaborate and they ultimately serve as a contractual agreement.

Is having a distinctive style as important to you, a graphic designer, as it is for an illustrator?

Having a style helps you get known. It is also a commodity that can be sold. But more important than having a personal style is being aware of other existing styles. These days clients are rather savvy about design: they know what's in and out and they know what they like. Therefore, it's important for a designer to be conscious of what's going on. Read all the magazines to find out what designers are doing around the world. It's good business; it allows for the competitive edge.

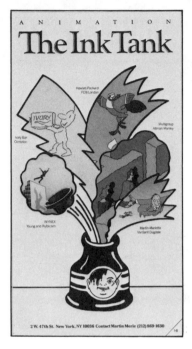

A N I M A T I O N

The Ink Tank

2 W. 47th St. New York, NY 10036 Contact Martin Merle (212) 869-1630

R. O. BLECHMAN, in addition to being an illustrator and cartoonist, is proprietor of The Ink Tank, an animation studio based in New York.

In addition to your work as an illustrator, The Ink Tank gives you the opportunity to do commercial and personal work on the same premises. How do you structure this business?

The studio is very flexible. I usually have a core of twelve to fifteen people who handle commercials, the bread-and-butter of the operation. The caviar is the occasional television special, which usually requires about thirty people.

Do you hire only animators, or designers and illustrators as well?

There are very few animators who are both accomplished artists and actors, as they have to be in order to act out the characters. So most of the hiring is not for animators but for people who design materials and render the materials to be animated.

How do you recruit people?

I usually ask illustration and animation instructors if they have any geniuses in their classes. I'm not so interested in what they've done as what I sense they can do, which takes a certain amount of intuition on my part.

They don't really need animation experience. For example, I hired someone a while ago who was a terrific graphic designer with a good eye and good head, but who had no experience as an illustrator or animator. He's developed a nice feeling for film and has become a mainstay of the studio.

Do you look at portfolios on a drop-off basis or do you meet with the prospective employees?

I like to see them personally because very often the meeting tells me as much about them as the work does. But my time is getting very limited these days, so I have to look at portfolios more and more on a drop-off basis.

Do you offer entry-level positions?

What I usually do is start people off as a messenger/apprentice, and invariably they work into the studio as an assistant manager, designer, or renderer. Usually I like to keep the categories fluid, because I don't like the idea of people just doing one thing.

Even if animation is not the ultimate goal, it seems that your studio is a good place to get professional experience. And for the would-be animator, it sounds like the perfect place. But what would you advise to those who cannot get a job with The Ink Tank?

Make films. Don't go to any studio classes. And don't let discouragement be crippling.

HENRIETTA CONDAK was formerly an art director at Columbia Records. She is now the principal of Condak Design, a small design studio located in New York City.

You left a large corporation that did very specific design to start your own studio. What is the most profound difference between working for yourself and working for others?

I still do work for others, but they are my clients whom I see from time to time. Now I don't have to get caught up in office politics. Time has a completely different meaning. I can accomplish much more in one day than I could in a week at CBS. Another important distinction is my ability to diversify. Until recently I had an established identity as a record album designer. Now I'm doing a wide range of projects.

Is the business side of your studio as fruitful as the creative side?

I have found it interesting to learn how to run a creative business. All of the things that I never had to concern myself with while I was working in a large corporation need my attention as much as the creative side. I spend a lot of time keeping track of studio expenses, billing, and budgets, but I really don't mind.

Your studio is comparatively small—just you and an assistant. How did you go about setting up your situation?

The main problem was finding affordable space. It is so difficult to find anything reasonable in Manhattan. I did not want a huge overhead, because I wasn't sure which direction I would be going in or if I'd even like the idea of being in business for myself. I was therefore lucky to find a shared space that was affordable. I slowly began to fix it up— painting, repairs, et cetera. Then I was faced with the problem of buying furniture, supplies, and a stat machine, which I did over the course of six months to a year. I've gotten the studio to where it is now comfortable and efficient for two people.

Do you want the business to get any larger?

I don't really know how big I want it to get, but I do see a steady rate of growth.

What will determine whether or not you expand your operation?

If I got a call from someone who wanted me to do a major project, and the only way I could do it was to bring in more people, I probably would have to do that if the situation looked semipermanent. But I kind of play it by ear. I like keeping my overhead low, because I can pick and choose my jobs. That ultimately allows me to keep the quality of my work high. It's important for a studio to have its own special image, and so I'm attempting to build that image.

Do you do any self-promotion?

I try to enter shows. That's the best kind of exposure. Otherwise, most of my work comes from word of mouth.

Do you hire temporary help to ease some of the work load?

As I need it. Having been in the business for so long I know who is available, or I ask friends for recommendations. But I find that my assistant and I can pretty much cover most of the work that comes up.

Having made a courageous leap from one business "life-style" to another, what would you advise about starting anew?

I would say that one shouldn't be afraid to make a change. Making the decision is the hardest part. After that commitment, it's relatively easy.

ANDRZEJ DUDZINSKI, a native of Warsaw, Poland, was invited to the United States in 1977 to attend the Aspen Conference. In 1978 he moved to New York City, where he works as an illustrator. His unique, surreal graphics conformed to the needs of the editorial illustration market, specifically for such newspapers as the *New York Times* and the *Boston Globe* and for magazines including *The Atlantic, Science '86, Playboy*, and *Texas Monthly*. Since 1982 he has been teaching an illustration portfolio class at Parsons School of Design in New York City.

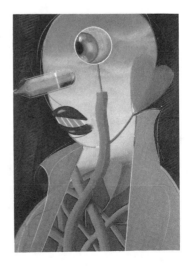

Why, in your mind, is a good portfolio necessary?

Survival. It's the basic tool of an illustrator. In my class I not only review the students' portfolios myself, but I invite art directors to help them out. I also invite other illustrators who show them their own portfolios, so the students have some means of comparison.

What do you look for in a portfolio?

I look for ideas. Since I am not an art director I don't look for published work; that's not as important to a student as diversity of thought and, of course, creativity.

Do you prefer a certain order or flow in a portfolio?

I improvise with every person. First I look at their work and try to bring it into some logical order according to their specific strengths. I have no rules for how a portfolio should look, but I don't think that a hodgepodge shows off their talents in the best light.

Should the student show various stages of development, from sketch to finish?

It's always interesting to see original work, but my feeling is that professional portfolios are usually composed of finished pieces. It just takes too long to go through books of sketches and roughs. And besides, most art directors want the security of seeing that someone else has already used the work before.

What do you think is the best type of promotion for someone just starting out?

I make my students create a booklet showing a good selection of their work. It should be intriguing and preferably involve some kind of a story. I believe it's more permanent than a simple mailer.

My advice is very simple. Be outstanding and

leave an everlasting impression through your creativity and ideas. I believe that ideas are the most important part of the initial development—more important than style. I always tell my students to strive for individuality. Do not fit into existing patterns or follow in someone else's stylistic footsteps.

JUDY FENDELMAN is chairman of the Illustration Department at Parsons School of Design in New York and runs her own design studio.

Tell me honestly, is school really necessary for an illustrator or designer?

When students talk to me about whether they should withdraw from school because they are getting some freelance or part-time work, I urge them to stay. I believe that if someone has graduated, it says he or she can hand in work on time, can work independently, and is disciplined. Getting a degree requires all these skills. So, in addition to the actual learning process, the degree sends out many positive signals.

What are your guidelines to students about portfolio presentation?

A portfolio has to show some kind of consistency, point of view, and style. I tell the student that if a portfolio tells *one* thing, it will be remembered; if it tells *two* things it may be remembered; if it tells *three* things, it will never be remembered.

So a portfolio should have a single focus?

More than that, it should be *clear*. And it is easier to say one thing clearly than say five. Some veteran illustrators thrive on their diversity; others make their livings by being able to imitate any style. But when most art directors see a student portfolio that is all over the map, they view it as untrustworthy.

Should students show their school projects as portfolio samples?

That's basically all they have. But there should be limits on what and how they show. A student is usually attached to the thing itself and doesn't understand that an illustration is only something made for the camera; until it is reproduced it is not an illustration. Moreover, a portfolio piece should never be intended to hang on a wall, so the fewer frames, mounts, and mattes, the better, since that type of presentation betrays the student's inexperience. My preference is for slide portfolios.

What is the optimum format for a beginner's portfolio?

Small is better. One ought to be able to carry it comfortably. But more important, many art directors have the same experience I had of working in a small office without large tables. I hated opening some giant portfolio and having twenty things fall out.

Once the material is organized neatly should there be any order or pacing?

Play your strong suit first. Group things together, because art directors think in those terms. If you work in black-and-white and color, put all the black-and-white and color in separate groupings. Pieces reading vertically should be grouped together, as should those reading horizontally, so that the art director doesn't have to continually turn them around. It is a professional courtesy, but makes the work more accessible too.

Should only finished work go into the initial portfolio?

No. When I look at a portfolio I want to see the thought process; I'm less interested in technical proficiency. The thought process and problem-solving skill are everything. A good idea will shine through an immature technique, but no amount of slick technical ability will hide an empty concept. As an art director, when I would hire an illustrator, I wanted someone who could solve the problem better than I could. Although I could think up twenty-five ideas a day, they wouldn't be twenty-five excellent ideas.

Do you think that all students should take their portfolios around immediately after graduating?

Not unless they feel secure in the ability to actually complete a professional assignment. The emotional fallout from failing is too serious. At Parsons we graduate students in May, and I see them again in September for review. The most common answer to the question, "What are you doing?" is, "I'm getting my book together." That's not a bad answer, but along with that should be an understanding of what they are up against. Success in this business has as much to do with dealing with an art director as it does with talent. The real test is not being able to read a manuscript and come up with a solution, but proving the ability to work with other people—which is a skill. If one doesn't feel confident, there's no point.

Do you encourage your illustration students to study graphic design?

Yes. The more one knows the better. I've heard too many kids say, "My first printed piece was a beautiful painting, but the art director really screwed it up by sticking ugly type on it." Well, knowing design won't help you influence the designer, but it will help you make constructive suggestions—perhaps more so if you understand the printing process, because one then has the skills to make a picture that will not suffer on press. After all, some colors are fugitive; some combinations are hard to reproduce. A lot of kids at Parsons work in pencil without any idea that it is hard to reproduce a pencil drawing in print.

What are your views about graduate school?

In four years (and sometimes Parsons does it in three) a student can be made ready for the marketplace on some level. I don't believe that illustration requires graduate work. It's always good to study more, and drawing is something that one has to do for a lifetime. If graduate school will help, fine, but I doubt it.

What are some of the pointers you give to your graduating students?

There is no point in entering the profession if it's not fun or satisfying—deeply satisfying. But, more important, I counsel them not to let themselves be abused. I do role-playing with the students in an interview situation, and I tell them that they have to know in advance what their tolerance is for abuse.

What do you mean by abuse?

I tell them not to work on spec, for example; I don't think one needs to do that. It is really disheartening for students to do something on the chance that if the art director likes it, it *might* be used. It's demeaning to the student if the same assignment is given to five other people as a kind of sweepstakes. However, it's different if the issue is approached graciously; if it is handled like a test. It's fair, for instance, if an art director offers a newcomer a piece that might have already run because he or she is interested to see how this artist will improve upon the existing solution. It just has to be couched correctly.

I tell students that they should judge the nature of a job. And I tell them how not to take it if they feel uncomfortable with it. *Dignity* is an important word. Since one is in this business for the long haul, personal ground rules should be established. This is a hard concept to get across to students. They're so anxious, so desperate, they want confirmation. If they get involved with a sympathetic art director, that's fine. But if they run up against somebody who gets off on being abusive, they should be aware of what's happening. It's only one part of doing business—but it's an important part.

LOUISE FILI is the art director of Pantheon Books, a division of Random House. She also teaches a portfolio class for graduating seniors at the School of Visual Arts in New York City.

What, for you, is the function of a portfolio?

The goal of the portfolio is to land a job. What I try to do in my portfolio class is give a range of assignments so that the students can decide which design area they're most interested in and which, therefore, should be emphasized in the portfolio. It's preferable to a potpourri and gives the art director the idea that the student has some sense of what he or she is doing and that there may even be a certain level of competence.

Since I use a lot of illustration for book jackets I spend most of my time looking at illustration portfolios. What I look for most is some kind of personal statement. Like most art directors who see many portfolios, I find it impossible to remember an artist unless there is a certain continuity throughout the book—perhaps it is a consistent style or a unique way of thinking. Too many portfolios are designed with every page showing a different style. Although it's possible to find a spark of inspiration in one of these, it would be difficult to feel confident about giving that illustrator a job. I want to be assured that they are going to continue doing the same type of work—at least in the initial stages of our relationship.

Diversity, however, can be a plus if the illustrator is basically a stylist. There are a few terrific illustrators who can do many different styles, and they are very useful if I have a preconceived idea for a jacket that requires one of their "looks." But, more often than not, the illustrator who has vision, who can think on his feet, and who can solve difficult problems with atypical symbols is the most valuable.

The same can be said for the reminder that is left behind. If it's going to be only one piece that the art director will hang up or put in a folder, then it should be something that somehow sums up the portfolio.

Do you believe that all portfolio work should be published, or at least look publishable?

Whether the work in the portfolio is published or not depends on one thing: its strength. Many beginners are so anxious to have a published piece that they'll put in anything, even the junk. Of course, published pieces are more impressive and give the insecure art director a certain confidence. However, good student work should not be scoffed at. Whatever proves that someone can solve problems and knows how to work within the constraints of the real world is a plus.

There are some schools of thought that say students (and professionals for that matter) should show tissues, comps, or thumbnails. I rarely find them very instructive. For those art directors who even look at portfolios there is a limited time frame to work in. Seeing a finished piece is more than enough. Moreover, students will typically say something like, "And this was for an assignment where we were supposed to take a map of the United States and cut it into ten pieces." I don't really care. If it's not self-explanatory, then it shouldn't be in there.

Should portfolios be generalized? For example, if

*someone wants to be a book jacket designer, should
there be examples in the book? Or is it enough
merely to show good design?*

I often see students or newcomers who say they
really want to do book jackets but who do not have
any samples in their portfolios. I stress that if
they're interested in doing jackets, not only should
they do sample jackets, but they should just totally
immerse themselves in the field. When I was first
interested in doing jackets I went to bookstores and
looked at everything that was being done and
everything that was historically important. It allowed me to judge which publishers would be most
sympathetic to the kind of work I wanted to do.
Otherwise it's just hit-or-miss.

*You work with many illustrators. Do you like them
to have at least a basic knowledge of type and
design?*

I prefer working with illustrators who can do their
own typography. I've always believed that all illustrators have an innate sense of typography, but they
are just afraid of it. If they are really resistant, I'll
either suggest a type treatment or actually set the
type for them and lay it out, but then have them
render the type as part of the illustration.

*At work and in school you see both student and
professional portfolios all the time. Do you critique
them?*

Some art directors do not critique portfolios and
just say yes, no, or maybe. I try to be as helpful as
possible, but it depends on the attitude of the person showing the portfolio. If he or she seems genu-
inely interested in knowing what I think and will
ask me for my detailed criticism, I will go through
the portfolio piece by piece.

Portfolios should be paced so that there is some
kind of continuity where you go from either one

91

type of illustration to another, or one form of design to the next. Most people have difficulty doing that. It's hard to be objective about your own portfolio, so sometimes it's better to have someone else help arrange it.

Are there requisites for the presentation of a portfolio, that is, any dos and do nots?

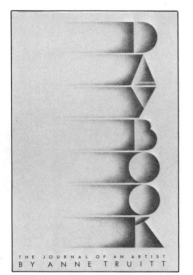

THE JOURNAL OF AN ARTIST
BY ANNE TRUITT

Regarding physical preparation there's a continuing debate on the subject of lamination. I try to encourage my students to laminate rather than put the work in those common loose-leaf binders with the sheets. Student work usually comes in all different sizes anyway, and it doesn't quite work in binders. Since lamination can be expensive I tell them to do the next best thing: flush mount all the pieces with acetate around them and put them in some kind of box. Then you have all different sizes, but at least there is some uniformity in the way they're presented.

How should people act when coming in for an appointment?

I think that there's enough flexibility in our field for anybody to come in any way, but attitude is very important. I don't like it when artists come in who are very aggressive. I've had some real terrorist illustrators come by who will not leave the office until I give them a job. They don't understand that when the time is right, it happens; and sometimes it takes years for the time to be right. There are others who think that the only way for me to remember them is if they keep calling in every couple of days, which I find extremely annoying. What I usually recommend is just to keep in touch with me through the mail. Mailers are very good reminders. And very often I will get a new mailer that fits the job on my desk.

You not only work for a corporation but you free-

*lance quite a bit. How do you feel about freelance
versus full-time employment?*

The freelance life is one breed of animal; the full-
time life is quite different and should be carefully
explored and understood. Very often one gets bur-
ied in corporations the size of Random House. But
there are many scenarios. I was at Random House
for several years as a freelance designer, which was
a nice position but was really dead-ended. I would
work until the book I was doing was finished and
then I was back on the street again. So I decided to
take a full-time job with Herb Lubalin to get a
range of experiences, but specifically to do book
jackets. Then, just by chance, I found myself back
at Random House again at the time that there was
an opening for an art director. If I had known that
it was available, it probably would never have occurred to me to apply. If I had taken my career de-
tour in a design studio, I'm sure I would never
have been considered for the job. So, very often it
is necessary to be a little bit more inventive with
your career and see if there are certain gaps that
must be filled in order to get the range of experience that will ready you for a higher position.

*Is there one bête noire of design, a problem that af-
fects neophytes, for example, that you have experienced through teaching and art directing?*

The thing I find in teaching or dealing with young
people that is most unfortunate is that very few
have a sense of design or illustration history. All
they know is what's been done now and maybe two
years ago. And it's not their fault. It's not something that was ever really emphasized in the
schools. It's hard to find books on the history of design. I try to include that as part of my curriculum
whenever possible, just so they get more of a sense
of it.

STEVEN GUARNACCIA is a freelance illustrator working in New York City. His clients include many national magazines and newspapers and he has illustrated numerous books, book jackets, annual reports, and advertisements. He is a consulting art director for Altman and Manley, an advertising agency in Boston.

When you began nine years ago, why did you decide to become a freelancer instead of getting a full-time job?

Being a freelancer means that every week is totally different; and that was the greatest appeal then and now. I'm convinced that, unless one has to do it for financial reasons, taking a full-time job is the worst way to get started as an illustrator. It fixes you too much in space and time. The greatest benefit of the freelance life is being a floater.

For example, the first couple of years I personally took my portfolio to all appointments. I had the time and the freedom and so never needed an agent. As it turned out, those personal contacts were important. In a sense, my office was every art director's office in New York. Sometimes they'd come to my studio, which was a corner of my apartment. This enabled me to establish a thread of contacts throughout the city. If I were sitting alone in a studio or working for someone else all day, I'd get a fixed focus, with contacts being limited to those people I worked with.

Another important factor for me at the time was the *New York Times*; it was a great gathering place—almost like the docks in *On the Waterfront*. One could commiserate with other illustrators, compare notes about art directors, and learn where the opportunities were. It was the nicest form of networking; we'd just sit around together, either working on jobs or waiting for one to be assigned. I met most of my illustrator friends at the *New York Times*, and that is only possible in a freelance situation.

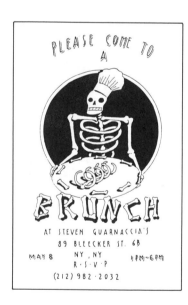

PLEASE COME TO A

BRUNCH

AT STEVEN GUARNACCIA'S
89 BLEECKER ST. 6B
MAY 8   NY, NY   II PM~6 PM
R·S·V·P
(212) 982·2032

Being a freelancer also meant that I could go to a museum in the middle of the week if I preferred to, because the weekends didn't hold sway over me. I must say that although I'm still a freelancer, my life has changed a bit. Now the weekend is a real weekend, and I tend to keep regular business hours even though there is no one making me do so.

What made you decide to set up your studio at home, rather than share office space with others?

I worked out of a room in my apartment because I tended to work, at least during the first few years, very long hours and very late. I was living my work: while I was eating dinner, I was thinking about the solution to the next assignment. My mind was never *not* on work, so mixing my business and home life made perfect sense. I now work in a studio separate from my home and I have an assistant come in a few days a week. But essentially I prefer to work alone. I know some people who have rented communal space, which has some benefits, including the sociability, but it would be difficult for me to function well in that situation.

When you began you had no training in, or sense of, business. How did you make it work?

I learned early on that the biggest problem with being a freelancer is cash flow. It takes time to get the money once a bill is presented, which means a system for meeting expenses is a necessity. When I began I would send out a bill every time I completed a job; now I send bills out at the end of each week. This regularized my business procedure and adequately covered the problem of cash flow. Of course, even at the outset I was getting assignments rather consistently; if one has ebbs and flows, then another method or some kind of cash reserve is necessary.

I've never used purchase orders or written contracts, except with advertising clients; I prefer to think that delivery of the work is my bond. It actually never occurred to me to give someone a contract; it hasn't been in keeping with the spirit of the job, and I don't think that I've ever been screwed because of this lack of procedure. In fact, I feel that I have established a kind of trust that must have helped my career along. Ultimately it is a matter of personal style.

From the outset you had a clear promotional strategy. Although you have never sent out the conventional mailers, you have done many clever cards. You also organized regular brunches in your studio, where artists and art directors would meet. How else did you promote yourself?

For one thing, every time I went into an art director's office, I was promoting—not in any conscious sense, but my presence went a long way to sell my work. In the beginning, before I had many printed jobs to show, I went to appointments with a portfolio full of ideas. That and my ability to discuss ideas in the presence of an art director showed that I could handle an editorial job.

I decided not to take out ads in the promotional books because I felt it was tacky to advertise myself in that way and, more importantly, I didn't have the money for it. Ultimately I really didn't respect the work I saw in those books. By and large, there's a lot of slick stuff that really doesn't interest me. What I did, though, was to send out a Christmas card every year or, when I went away on an extended vacation, which I did often, I'd send out illustrated cards to all of my clients letting them know that I was going away and when I'd be back. That was more like keeping in touch, although in retrospect I realize that it was a type of self-promotion. Now I opt for entering juried shows and trying to get my work into annuals. I also have come to see the value of advertising in illustrators' directories, especially for advertising clients.

Your early portfolio was idiosyncratic, but it clearly intrigued enough art directors to give you a try. Of course, once you had some published work it was easy for other art buyers to see your potential. Is there a strategy to preparing a good portfolio?

I have told students to follow their own intuition, to put their favorite work into a portfolio rather than the work that they think is going to get them jobs.

But actually more important than the portfolio, in my opinion, is staying in touch with the profession. Be on as many mailing lists as possible. I've joined a couple of professional organizations, such as the Graphic Artists Guild and, more significantly, the American Institute of Graphic Arts, which, for the most part, has graphic designers as members. That's what makes it an interesting organization; designers, of course, are the people who employ illustrators, so I joined to be in touch with what's going on with the other end of the business.

In addition to your other work, you have become an art director on an occasional basis. How does this help you as a freelance illustrator?

For three years I have been working with Altman and Manley as an illustrator. But, because there is a conceptual affinity between us, we thought that it would be a good idea if I started working with them as a consultant—coming up with ideas and initiating projects that would be given to other illustrators.

As a consultant, I'm still a freelancer. However, in this case, since I go up to Boston as often as once a week, it gives a certain coherence to an otherwise scattered professional life and helps me understand the profession in a broader context.

PHILIP HAYS is an illustrator and the chairman of the illustration department at Art Center College in Los Angeles, California.

Your school graduates a high number of very proficient illustrators each year. Their portfolios are usually conceptually well rounded and stylistically distinctive. What advice would you give for preparing a portfolio?

A student is not finished upon graduation from a school. We provide them with whatever they're going to need twenty years down the road, and the portfolio is the immediate tool.

What I look for in a portfolio and what is necessary are, perhaps, two different things. What is necessary is something that will get the work one wants to do. What I look for, however, is something that will, hopefully, shape the future of illustration. I'm interested in students who are on the leading edge—people such as Matt Mahurin or Jeff Smith. That's my personal goal and it is not for everyone.

Do you think that a portfolio should reflect a conceptual and stylistic single-mindedness?

It depends entirely on the illustrator. If one thing is done very well, then that's what the portfolio must show. The portfolio should be what you want to do and what you *like* to do. There should be nothing in it that you do not want to do, because if you show it to an art director, and he gives you an assignment based on something you're not comfortable with, you're trapped.

Do you have any opinion, pro or con, about including student projects in the portfolio?

Well, if you are a newly graduated student, that's what the portfolio has to be. At Art Center, the final three semesters are intense portfolio preparation periods. We have poster competitions for real clients, and these pieces are printed. The winner goes out with 100 posters to give away as promotion. Many times the posters are distributed internationally.

What should be included in an effective portfolio?

I don't think there should be more than twenty pieces, particularly if the work is very complicated. Art directors are bored beyond twenty. Ten or fifteen is plenty.

I recommend that illustrators show 8- by 10-inch transparencies. They're much more convenient to carry—especially in bad weather. Moreover, most art directors' offices are very cluttered. They just don't have room to spread the work out, so it's a practical matter. We also encourage showing one or two small originals, though.

The portfolio should not be arranged helter-skelter. There should be a deliberate pacing, starting with one big bang and, somewhere in the middle, another big bang, and ending with one too. The medium work is sandwiched in between.

Do you prep students on the way to act, look, and dress?

Well, short of being a slob, I don't think it's terribly important. Art directors certainly don't care. The work is the whole thing.

Do you encourage illustration students to study and practice graphic design?

Absolutely. Graphics is required. We have a minor for the people who are willing to go further. Those two disciplines go hand in hand and increase the possibility of getting work down the road.

With all the emphasis you place on the undergraduate, what are your thoughts about graduate school for illustrators? Does it improve their chances for success?

No. At least not for illustration students at Art Center; maybe for those at a different school. But my feeling is that New York City itself is the best master's program in the world! When students graduate after eight semesters, they are ready to go.

But Art Center does have a master's program, correct?

Ours is a two-year program. The student writes a thesis and works closely with a group of instructors and academic people. I think it's a bit redundant. But, as opposed to illustrators who are in business to work, painters usually end up teaching, and the degree ensures them more money. If an illustrator decides to teach, a degree is not necessary; rather, professional standing is the key.

Are there any advantages to staying in California after graduation?

Just the weather. That's *all*, believe me. The market in California is tough. There's actually a lot of work, but you have to drive thousands of miles just to find it. New York City is so central.

Moreover, New York is an international market. One can establish an international reputation very quickly, and a lot of Art Center graduates have done it, whereas I know some good illustrators in California who are really struggling.

If someone makes a reputation in New York do you think it is possible for him or her to return to California and do well?

Yes. Then one can do it anywhere—even Montana. But at that stage it is good to have a representative in New York. So the equation is live, work, and establish a reputation and get a rep in New York. Then, if you like, you can move any place.

Illustration is actually a great life. You can design your own life-style. The rewards of walking by a magazine stand and seeing your cover and knowing that a million people have it on their coffee tables are wonderful. It's communication on a grand scale.

WILL HOPKINS is a co-principal of the Hopkins Group, a design firm based in New York City that specializes in magazine consulting and art direction. Hopkins is the former art director of *Look* magazine, *American Photographer*, and *The Wharton Magazine*. He and his partner, Ira Friedlander, also serve as the art directors of *American Health* and *Mother Earth News*.

You run a comparatively small studio. . .

. . .That's right. There are four of us: myself and my partner, a studio manager, and an apprentice. We also employ a bookkeeper a few days a week.

You have worked on many magazines as a full-time art director. What is the difference between that approach and running an independent studio?

Our studio is a bit unorthodox because we don't do a lot of corporate work. From what I understand regular studios to be, people are assigned to certain jobs and their work is monitored by time cards and job sheets. We don't do that. We don't know how to and, what's more, we don't want to. My partner and I share in all the design work.

But, to answer your question directly, the differences between working inside a company and outside are mostly psychological. We work so closely with our clients over a long period of time that it's more or less like we are on staff. The only measurable difference is a certain added leverage in the decision-making process, because we are independent.

Well, if there is no significant difference between being on staff or on your own, why are you not sim-

ply on staff somewhere, which would avoid the costs of overhead?

We like to do many different things at the same time, and as full-time employees that would be out of the question.

Since you perform many different tasks during the course of a year, do you need to have freelance support?

Yes. We usually hire the mechanical people through word-of-mouth recommendations, because we want to be sure of who we get. But we also assign a lot of photography and illustration. For that we look at portfolios. For certain projects we also hire freelance editors and copy editors.

Is there room for advancement in your organization?

If we hire someone for pasteup who is also a good designer, we make every effort to advance them. For example, we are elevating someone in our freelance pasteup crew to the staff of *American Health*. But, conversely, if I'm looking for a paste-up person, I would hope that's what he or she wants to be. I don't go out of my way to make designers out of board people. However, a lot of the pasteup artists we use are young illustrators who are not yet earning money illustrating. In this case, if they are good, we try to give them illustration work.

Do you train designers as a rule?

We have an apprenticeship program, of sorts. They work with us for about two years and then we kick them out. It's healthy for designers to move around rather than stay with one studio for too long a period.

What is your definition of a good editorial designer?

I'll begin with a negative one. It is very difficult to find young people who are concerned about subject matter as opposed to how individual pages look. That, in my opinion, is a shallow form of design. In this era of specialization too many people are working on magazines for which interest in content has become irrelevant. I believe that if designers are going to grow they can't work against the subject. Design for design's sake is not part of editorial responsibility. Curiosity and commitment are terribly important to good design work.

TIBOR KALMAN is the principal of M&Co., a design studio based in New York City.

You have been in business for six years. How did you go about starting a studio and how would you advise others to do so?

This is one of the easiest businesses to start. If you open a pizza parlor, you've got to buy an oven, you've got to pay rent. If you decide to open a graphic design firm, you can do it with a pencil and a telephone. What you must have, though, are contacts with a little bit of work. Not a lot of work, mind you, because you couldn't do a lot by yourself. But a little is just fine to start.

I think most successful design studios are started in kitchens; some are started in living rooms and bedrooms, but basically they start at home.

The other wonderful thing is that there is an enormous amount of work to be had. Every person knows someone who can offer a little bit of design work. Sometimes it's just a sign for a store or a business card for a restaurant or a letterhead for a friend who is a writer. There are just mountains of little jobs out there that people can start off with.

Alexander Isley
M&Co.

212 243-0082
50 West 17th Street
New York, NY 10011

Danny Abelson

212 243-0082
50 West 17th Street
New York, NY 10011

Tibor Kalman
M&Co.

212 243-0082
50 West 17th Street
New York, NY 10011

Tibor Kalman
M&Co.

212 243-0082
50 West 17th Street
New York, NY 10011

Thomas Kluepfel
M&Co.

212 243-0082
50 West 17th Street
New York, NY 10011

That is good for the homebound entrepreneur, but what happens when you want to expand and rent space? Doesn't that get you into the world of high finance?

You have to be very cautious and take it very slowly. Of course, most people begin to outgrow the kitchen table and the easiest way to leave home is to rent space in someone else's studio. It's a fairly common practice because design studios tend to fluctuate in size as a result of the increase and decrease in the staff or freelancers. Many design studios are happy to rent out space for a finite period to offset a lack of seasonal work. That's a good way for people to get started.

The other way is to get involved with a group of two or three people and rent an inexpensive office. Of course, when you do that you have to deal with your first chunk of overhead—the rent. Things will never be the same afterward because you have a business expense that must be maintained regardless of whether you have a lot or a little work. It's something that can mushroom quickly from there. You have to be very cautious about it, because every time you add more overhead you have to make more profit, and that limits the type of jobs, the number of jobs, and the amount of time you can spend on those jobs.

Let us talk a little about image. The most important aspect is a name. What factors are important in choosing one?

As far as picking a name goes, there are two schools of thought. One is where the firm is named after the principal; the other sort of name is distinctive and suggestive of something relating to the studio. Actually, there might be a third group of names that do not mean anything and are often kind of quirky. That's what we set out to do when establishing M&Co. We wanted a name that sounded like a firm—thus the "and Company"—

but wasn't really like a firm; so we picked the letter *M*.

Well, the "and Company" suggests that you have incorporated. Once out of the kitchen and into the real world, is it good to do that?

I'm not an expert, but I'm aware of two reasons why people incorporate. One is that it buys a certain amount of protection from creditors. For example, while James Smith is responsible for James Smith's debts, James Smith is not responsible for the debts of James Smith, Inc. That's the great American practice called the "corporate veil," which insulates individual owners of corporations against liabilities of the corporation. Therefore, if you're buying, let's say, $10,000 worth of printing on behalf of a major client and it turns out poorly, and the client says "We're not paying for it," and the printer defends the quality and demands his money, your corporation legally protects you from being personally responsible. On another level incorporation is important because it offers tax benefits that are unavailable to individuals.

I believe that the decision to incorporate or not is between the designer and the accountant. Therefore, it is not very useful to give general information on that subject. It's different for different cases.

You mentioned accountants. Is it important to have one? Or is it better to retain a lawyer?

I think people overstate the extent to which they need lawyers. M&Co. does not employ a lawyer on a daily basis for normal relations with clients. We use lawyers when there's trouble, but the normal, day-to-day procedures only require a reasonable amount of expertise on the part of the designer regarding how to write a good contract. And the Graphic Artists Guild provides that kind of expertise. The American Institute of Graphic Arts offers a sample form, as does the Society of Typographic Arts.

Consider the next stage. The designer has chosen a name, has dealt with an accountant and/or a lawyer, and is now ready to move into his or her own space. What pointers would you offer for designing that space?

Usually the first requisite is that there be a lot of flat or tabletop space. Whatever flat space you have you'll use. The second most important factor is good light—a good mix of natural and fluorescent light.

When designers are working at their boards or at their desks, they need to be isolated from other people. That way, I think, when someone walks across the room, or someone walks into the room, there is no distraction. In our office we use low wall partitions (about 4 1/2 feet high), so that if you stand up you can speak across the top, but if you are sitting there is no disturbance.

What about furniture?

People always overstate how many flat files they need. Flat files are an incredibly expensive way to store materials, both in terms of space and the cost of the files themselves. Flat files should only be used for active job storage, not for dead storage. The finished work should be packed flat and stored on shelves.

M&Co. has done a series of wonderful, imaginative promotions. What is your philosophy about this?

The first thing that must be said about self-promotion is that the best form is no self-promotion. The best job is the one for which you're referred by word of mouth—by a colleague or another client. It's better because there is already, on the part of the person who is referred to you, a sense of trust.

Trust and faith are the most positive results of a professional referral. It is the graphic designer's coin of the realm.

We do, however, have a very specific and straightforward self-promotion program. It evolved from a simple Christmas card that we kept playing with throughout the years. The card grew into an object which was sent as a gift. But in addition to being a link with past, present, and future clients, we used it as a means of demonstrating our design ability and sense of humor to clients and colleagues. Every year we send out an expensive Christmas promotion that cannot help but raise some eyebrows.

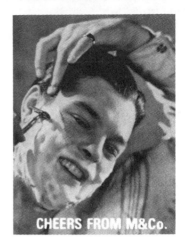

The best was our first: a series of chocolate *M's*. We struggled to find someone who would cast the chocolates for us. In the second year we sent out cookies in a tin; of course, once the cookies were eaten the box was too nice to throw away. We got clients specifically from that promo.

The other thing that is important to remember is not to be conservative about spending money on these things, because the potential return on the investment is enormous. If you spend as much as $3,000 to $5,000 on a promotion, all you need is one client to come from it to recoup the cost.

Speaking about money, do you have a billing method that is worth sharing?

We bill every job every month. Even if the job is not completed, we bill for the finished portion every month. That's one thing that has caused major improvement in our cash flow. This process also helps to avoid any honesty problems that the client may have. Chances are, if you have problems in the beginning of the billing, you're going to have problems all the way through.

Bills should always be typed on a letterhead; I don't believe in billing forms. One should be meticulous about the wording of bills. Think very carefully about the wording above the price, because that's really going to have a major influence on the person who has to approve the bill. And don't forget that every person who approves a bill has a boss who also has to approve the bill. So, it has to look right, it has to read right, it has to be neat, it has to look professional.

You hire young people for M&Co. If you are originally hiring for a pasteup position is there room for advancement? Do you encourage growth? And do you prefer to hire people with experience or are you willing to train on the job?

I have hired people with absolutely no experience and I have hired those with tons. I have found some people with no experience to be brilliant and I have found experienced designers who stink. So I don't think that there is any rule of thumb. It's clear that most people have to start in this business at a pasteup level, but I think that there's a tremendous amount of design work and decision making that's done at a pasteup level. There's room for opportunity at all levels.

In Germany young architects are required to spend their summers working on construction sites, laying bricks and framing buildings. I think that's what the pasteup position is to a designer. One really has to get into the trenches and pasteup folios, go down to the printer and screw around with things. That's the best way to learn the language of design.

MICHAEL KLEIN is a freelance illustrator living in New York City. Until recently he was an assistant to the illustrator Steven Guarnaccia.

Did you always want to study illustration?

Originally I studied business, marketing, and advertising. I got a B.S. in economics, specifically in marketing. I wanted to work in advertising, combining the creative with the business expertise, but I decided that I was getting too involved in the business part. I quit, feeling that I had to explore the creative side of myself.

What did you do next?

At twenty-three years old, I went to Parsons School of Design where I studied illustration for a year. Then I got a job as an assistant to Steven Guarnaccia.

How did that come about?

While I was at Parsons I had a job in the illustration office. Steven called one day looking for an assistant. As fate would have it, I happened to answer the phone and suggested myself for the position. I got it, and it worked out so well that we continued the relationship for a year and a half.

Was this a full-time job?

When I started I still had a semester to go at Parsons, so I worked part-time. I worked full-time during the summer and thereafter.

What were your responsibilities as an assistant?

The tasks varied. Most were not glamorous, but some were educational. I kept track of the billing, which sort of called upon my business skills. I sent out letters, answered the telephone, wrapped art, and sent it out. One of the more educational things was cutting overlays, since I could work on technique and speed. Once or twice I inked a drawing. It wasn't often, since Steven's hand is very important for the finished art. We did, however, work together on some projects where I actually helped come up with concepts. He used me to generate a lot of ideas and then would edit them. The process would help him get his own wheels turning.

Were you already good with conceptual thinking?

My ideas weren't polished, but I think this process helped fine-tune my thinking.

How did the experience of working and going to school help you creatively?

The most important thing was that the schedule was very flexible. If something came up, or I felt that I needed an extra day to work on my own projects, then the hours were more flexible than any other full-time job. Working at Steven's also gave me a place to get intelligent and intense feedback. Moreover, the whole environment was creatively stimulating. I got to meet other illustrators and I was able to watch Steven's process.

He also has an incredible library, so that whenever I had a particular illustration problem to solve, I could look at books and see how it was handled in the past. Not even the school was so well equipped.

Is this what you expected the job to be like?

I went into the job hoping that it would be that way. If I hadn't had the opportunity to work on my own stuff and have time-flexibility, it would have been a lot less interesting. I don't think that I would have stayed as long as I did.

During your year-and-a-half stint, did you take your portfolio around on interviews and dropoffs?

Yes. I went out on two passes. One of the good things about the job, however, was that if I felt that I wasn't getting anywhere, I had the opportunity to reconsider my portfolio without feeling that I had to make a living right away.

What was the initial response to your work?

The response was positive and encouraging. Art directors told me that they liked certain concepts. I felt that they could see I had something below the surface, and that was satisfying. But I didn't get any work from the first time I went around. Something was preventing people from taking the chance.

Do you know what it was?

Well, I know that my portfolio had a wide variety of styles. I was in an experimental phase where I was checking out everything, looking for an approach that felt comfortable. I had to figure out what was liked and disliked, basically, and figure out how to create a style or formulate an approach that would allow what was liked to come through in my work.

How did that come about?

By continuing to work and look. I think the answer was in the portfolio, and by going back to look at it I was able to figure out the proper route. Since there were so many different pieces in there, some were getting better responses than others. I listened intently to all comments.

When I finally started to get a few jobs, the work itself provided an answer. I had to work on a fast deadline and come up with a solution, and somehow the natural approach came through.

Did Guarnaccia's graphic style rub off on you?

Certainly. His work gave me an indication of how to veer away from what I was doing as a student. There was a time when my work looked very similar to Steven's. I remember sitting down to work on my own jobs and thinking, I have to create a professional piece. What does a professional piece look like? I was very familiar with Steven's work, which to me was very professional. So I had to get to the point where I had the confidence to see my work as professional too. Gradually I moved through the mimicry stage. Now I feel that I'm continuing to move towards the Michael Klein stage.

Since you were in the studio all the time, were you able to pick up assignments on the rebound, so to speak?

There were occasions when that was the case. A job would come through that Steven couldn't do, and when he felt that it was appropriate he would recommend me. In general it worked out very well. The art directors who took the recommendations would call me and ask to see samples. Very often I got the job. In fact, I would say that was one of the real advantages of being an assistant.

CHERYL LEWIN runs her own design studio in New York City.

You spent four years working in design studios. How much of that experience came in handy when you started your own firm?

When I started I worked for four different studios—one a year. They were good places doing very good work. First and foremost, I learned about the business of design. Doing good work is just part of the equation. You have to wear many hats, and learning to juggle the responsibilities and change hats quickly is the greatest asset. This is something that one can only learn from experience.

What if beginning designers can get only a lowly job at a studio?

I think that it's important to start in a job where you respect the people. Such a place is valuable, even if you have to sweep the floors, because there's something positive in the air and the contacts you get from those first jobs will stay with you forever. So it doesn't really matter what you're doing, although if you are lucky enough to get a very responsible position right away, so much the better. The main thing is to develop good habits, because the bad ones will be hard to lose.

One of the habits you seem to have acquired is a good billing sense. What are some of your pointers for not losing your shirt in the early stages of business?

Billing is an uncomfortable area, but one of the things that makes billing, or any client relationship, easier is to make sure that you have everything in writing in an initial proposal. Billing is just the fulfillment of that agreement. You must be as thorough as possible at the outset, because when the project is just beginning, everyone is optimistic: the client really needs you, so you're in a good negotiating position.

From your experience, what are some of the most important items to include in a proposal?

Most are very obvious, yet it is tempting to leave them out. Something as simple as sales tax, for instance, *should* be indicated. It's a considerable chunk of money. Moreover, it may be a legal necessity, not a personal whim. Also, simple items like shipping and delivery charges should be included for printed materials, et cetera. The rule of thumb is to make certain all items, no matter how large or small, are accounted for, so you don't lose money.

NONNIE LOCKE, an artists' representative, is a partner in the John Locke Studio in New York City.

Why should illustrators have an agent?

One reason is that there are so many good illustrators out there nowadays. It's very tough for a new-

comer to bang on doors and hope to be seen. Art directors simply don't have the time to see everyone and so they often prefer to work, at least initially, through an agent. The other reason is it leaves the artist much more time to do the work, which is presumably what they really want to do.

You represent some very well established illustrators and cartoonists in the United States and Europe, including Edward Gorey, Ronald Searle, and André François. With this illustrious stable your criteria for new artists must be very strict. What do you look for?

We would rather have an artist who is not for everyone than one who does work like everyone else because it is in vogue at the moment. The artists we are interested in are those who can complement an author's text through interpretation rather than simply illustrate the author's words verbatim. Artists are free spirits and therefore should be allowed to express themselves.

What services do you, or for that matter most artists' representatives, offer a client?

Everything. We show the work. We have the personal contacts with art directors and designers. We arrange the price structure. And, of course, we do the billing.

What suggestions do you have for the newcomer who is looking for a representative?

Many reps look at portfolios even though they are not taking people on. If they see someone who is really smashing they can advise them on who to see, perhaps even make a direct recommendation.

The Society of Illustrators and other artists' societies usually have good recommendation services. Also, directories, such as the *Art Director's Index,* have lists of all the representatives in the field. I suggest that one just call around and check on the reputations of the prospective agents before committing oneself.

You must see many portfolios. What are your dos and do nots?

The most self-defeating thing about student portfolios is that they tend to contain everything the student has ever done. My previous point about art directors applies to agents too: there just isn't enough time. I prefer to see strength in one area as opposed to someone who is versatile. Although I know that's hard for someone just out of school, I think that it should be a goal.

RICHARD MANTEL, a former art director for CBS Records and Push Pin Studios, runs a one-person illustration and design studio in New York City.

As an illustrator and designer do you combine your talents into one practice or do you sell each separately?

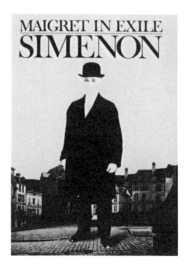

In some cases they overlap. For example, when I do book jackets or posters, the two disciplines are required simultaneously. I do other work, however, that calls for straight art direction, such as the "advertorials" that I do for *New York* magazine. In such a situation I will hire an illustrator other than myself.

Is it advantageous to have both skills?

It gives me an advantage in terms of knowledge and, of course, in terms of my earning potential. However, it is very difficult to do both at the same time, except with something small, like a book jacket. It is too emotionally draining. If I am art directing a large project that requires multiple illustrations, I just wouldn't have the emotional equipment to handle both.

In terms of selling your wares, do you separate illustration from design?

I have an agent for illustration work, so work comes in by itself, so to speak. The design work I handle on my own.

I've had the majority of my design clients for a long time, mostly in publishing; I really don't need to solicit too much in that area. They know me, so they just call when they need me. In addition, the access to work is quite different for design than for illustration. For the latter you may be working directly for an art director or a design studio. For design you're more likely to be working with an art buyer, the head of production at some agency, or the editor of a publication.

Do you think it is better to deal with your design clients yourself?

I'm not sure. I've never tried soliciting design work through an agent. I find that clients tend to need more one-on-one attention for design work. There is more ongoing servicing necessary in the course of a design project. With illustration, corrections or adjustments can be handled through the agent.

Running a one-person studio without any freelance help, are you limited in the amount of work you can take on? Do you lose accounts?

I don't turn down jobs and I don't do my own board work either. I use a very good production studio for mechanicals. This means that I do not have to carry a large overhead when all I'm doing are illustrations. But when I have a larger project that involves doing a design format and following it through with type and mechanicals, I hire the production studio on a job-to-job basis.

You have said that you do freelance art direction as well as design and illustration. What is it about art direction that has a special interest for you?

Having once been an art director, and having to deal with art directors as an illustrator, sometimes not happily, it's nice to have total control of a job from beginning to end. I enjoy matching the right illustrator with the right job and seeing satisfying results.

Many people who work for themselves have at least an assistant or two. What are the basic problems with working alone?

I cannot delegate any part of my illustration work. Everything involved is my time. Also, as an illustrator, the basic problem for me is the isolation of the process. It's hard to sit by the board with brush in hand, alone, day after day. It's very enervating for me, which is exactly why I like to balance illustration with design. It gives me a chance to get out and to deal with people. It also demands a different kind of discipline that yields a different kind of satisfaction. Design can be done with the help of others and does not require that total time commitment. Of course, the other side of that coin is the ability to turn out a terrific picture that has never existed before in any form. The solitude is then offset by the satisfaction.

Do you feel that your career is limited in any way by the path you have chosen?

I would like to get more corporate work than I do now. I'm not sure if that's an inherent limitation in the way my business has evolved, but I don't seem to have many access points for that kind of work.

I'd like to do more logos, annual reports, and packaging. My steady accounts are more "editorial": magazines, book jackets, record jackets, and posters.

Is there a methodological difference between an illustrator and designer?

Being an illustrator takes a particular kind of sensibility. It's not just the long hours, which are hard enough, or the isolation, which is also difficult. It's like being a cab driver, where you're sitting at the curb and no one is in the car and you wonder if anyone's ever going to show up. The next minute, someone hops in, and you're rushing off to the airport. The illustrator sits around waiting for the phone to ring. He thinks no one else is ever going to call. Then all of a sudden the phone rings and he's up two or three nights trying to make a short deadline. One really has to have the kind of sensibility that can handle that kind of pressure and that kind of working rhythm. I think it's much easier to manage time as a staff designer. It's a different kind of discipline, but one basically knows what the hours are going to be and that there's a paycheck every week. There is no freelance anxiety.

But what about the freelance designer? Are there not problems in that area too?

For me, the largest problem is broadening my base to attract different kinds of clients. I don't have the advantages that a large, high-profile studio would afford me.

Young designers should be cautious about freelancing too early in their careers. I think it's critical to work for someone from whom one can learn. I've seen many very talented people fail to live up to their potential. They essentially stopped learning by isolating themselves too soon after graduating from school. The first few years after graduation are the most important for creative growth.

BARBARA NESSIM is a veteran freelance illustrator, painter, and computer artist who lives in New York City. In 1980 she established the firm Nessim and Associates, where she collaborates with fellow illustrators on corporate and other projects. Her clients include many national firms and magazines.

You have been a freelancer for many years. Do you feel it has been a good way of life?

In many ways it has. It has allowed me certain freedoms, one of them being the time to work on my personal paintings and drawings. But everything has its plus and minus sides. One of the negatives in this business is that one has little or no control over income when one must wait to be contacted for a job. I have always kept enough money saved in order to live for six months without worrying. This is a *must* if you intend to work for yourself.

Do you really think that freelance illustrators are in an inferior position?

Reviewing the history of illustration, one cannot ignore the fact that the illustrators of the twenties, thirties, forties, and fifties held prestigious positions in society. Their incomes were commensurate with those of successful business people. However, the budgets for illustration today have diminished greatly since the sixties. I've seen it happen. For example, the page rate in the early sixties for an illustration in *Redbook* magazine used to be $1,200; in 1980, it was $800.

That said, what about the would-be illustrator? How should he or she break into the market? Is promotion important?

Very important! One must get around, show the portfolio, and meet art directors. Artists today have

119

a better means of promoting themselves. Black-and-white drawings can be beautifully reproduced for a fraction of what it cost in the past. Also, personal computers have made mailing lists easier to assemble.

More competitions exist than ever before. Although these are good promotional outlets, they can be expensive and time-consuming. You might enter ten drawings in one of them, spend $100 or more, and perhaps get one in, if you're lucky. If you are accepted then you have to pay a hanging fee for the honor. I always felt there was something ironic in that. The only book with no charge is *Graphis*, the Swiss design magazine.

There are also more promotional books—the annuals for which you pay to advertise. They are good because you can choose the art that is most representative. They are, however, very expensive, with the exception of *RSVP*—a good deal for the illustrator just starting out.

Should the young illustrator go directly into the marketplace or take an intermediary step?

My advice to an illustrator is to start at a company, agency, or design studio. If you want to do illustration, great, but if you learn about type and design as well, you will expand your potential markets. You'll also have a better understanding of art directors.

Where is the best place to set up shop?

Most illustrators work at home. My studio has been in my home for over twenty years. A lot of my work is done at night, so it's convenient to be in one place. Having a separate workplace isn't a bad idea, but it depends on your personal life and habits. If you rent space in an existing studio, you'll not only get exposure to other people, you might be able to work off the studio as well. For example, if the studio gets busy, it is more likely to give the extra work to you than to an outsider. It's a good way to get some work published and to raise surplus cash.

PAULA SCHER is a principal in Koppel and Scher, a design firm based in New York City. For ten years she was senior art director at CBS Records.

You teach a portfolio class for senior graphic design students. What do you think makes a great design portfolio?

The kind of portfolio that thrills me is one that either shows an incredible sense of humor or a lot of guts. Although a student's portfolio has got to have some business reality, if it's too business-oriented, it is invariably dull. I think that somebody who is twenty-one or twenty-two years old should be shocking and surprising me. I don't think that they should be doing work that's more tired than my own.

Do you look for diversity or single-mindedness?

Designers' and illustrators' portfolios are like apples and oranges. I look for single-mindedness with an illustrator. The biggest trap that illustrators fall—or are pushed—into is that they think they have to work in every style. It's confusing to the art director because it's impossible to anticipate what kind of work will come back. Conversely, with a designer it's important to do many things well and know how to approach a lot of different problems. On the other hand, a designer should beware of showing too many different design schools or movements in one portfolio. If I see something designed in the Swiss mode and then in a post-modern mode and then in a sort of Herb Lubalin mode, all in the same portfolio, I become confused. I wonder what

this designer is really trying to say, if anything. A designer should have a sense of history, but not be just a conduit of style.

How do you feel about published versus "comp" work in a portfolio?

Very often school projects are better than printed samples. I've run into terrific young designers who have awful professional work and excellent school work. This can happen because a good designer takes a bad job to meet expenses. It's better to put unprinted work in a book than to show the poor work. Erratic levels of work are confusing, because you don't know if the good work is an accident or not.

How should a portfolio be prepared?

The worst thing you can do is put a lot of acetate over the work, because it tends to yellow. A pet peeve of mine is the students who shoot slides of their work thinking that everything always looks a little bit better. I always feel that they are concealing a mistake or faking something. I'd rather see the whole thing right in front of me. They should accept the responsibility. If the work is good, the presentation is of secondary importance.

Do you like to see how someone came to the solution? Are progressives necessary?

I don't think it's necessary to show one's dirty underwear in public. In other words, why show tissues and thumbnails unless they are specifically requested? Some people like to see how others work. I don't care about the process. If it's good, that's good enough for me—unless it was stolen from somebody.

What do you consider to be the optimum number of pieces for a portfolio?

122

For a student, fifteen good pieces are better than twenty if five of them are mediocre. However, if there are only ten good ones, then show that number; if there are twenty-five great ones, show that.

The size of pieces should be whatever the problem calls for. For example, if it is a record cover, it should be 12 1/4 by 12 1/4 inches. If it's a magazine, it should be 8 1/2 by 11 inches, etcetera.

Do you think that comportment is an issue when someone shows a portfolio or hands in work?

Well, yes and no. Graphic artists are a weird breed. I think it's ridiculous to approach this profession the way an accountant or a lawyer approaches a job. I would be very suspicious of someone who was very well groomed and well behaved, because I would assume that that is more important than their work. On the other hand, I think the biggest problem that students have, and the one that turns me sour immediately, is the inability to articulate an issue. I don't think that that is a grooming problem, it's an education problem. Ultimately they'll have to talk to clients, so one wants to assume that they're going to be able to carry on an intelligent conversation and be able to write a letter, if need be.

The biggest problem that art directors and designers have is not one of dress or demeanor; it's more of a social issue. If one is extremely talented and never speaks, then he or she should get a rep. Conversely, another thing that annoys me is the student or neophyte who feels it's necessary to explain everything in the portfolio. If the work has to be explained, it probably means it's not very good.

How do you go about critiquing a portfolio?

It really depends on what the person is prepared to hear. Some people want to hear the truth; others don't. It's easy to tell. I am sensitive to the sensitive ones, but I prefer to be as forthright as possible.

You hire many of your own students for jobs in your studio. When you are hiring for a board job, for example, do you give them the opportunity to rise eventually to a higher design position?

Our studio is not a model for the profession. It's run very erratically: everybody does everything, from managing the accounts to sweeping the floor. When we have a lot of design work, then everybody gets to design. When we are not busy, then no one designs.

You recently made a major career change yourself, having left the security of a terrific job as art director of CBS Records to start your own studio. Why did you make the leap?

When I decided to leave the corporation I immediately became a freelancer and got some very good accounts. But after a while being a freelancer felt too insecure. I decided to form a studio, with the awareness that I did not want to be perceived as a freelancer with a little studio, but rather as a business that would do work with other businesses. So becoming a partnership was a positive way of presenting myself to corporate clients. Another reason that I formed the partnership, frankly, was that I didn't want to do this alone. Some people enjoy working with a few assistants; I don't. I also wanted a bigger environment in which to work, because I like to have a lot of jobs going on at once. I also find it invigorating to have people around. My work is better when I am collaborating or, at least, when I can show it to someone I respect for feedback.

Once you decided to start Koppel and Scher, did you set limits for your growth?

The problem with a larger situation is a larger overhead, which means greater responsibility to make billings. For someone just beginning, it's better to start out small. We did that initially, but the work we have been getting forced us to grow. Happily, I don't think that we're going to get very much bigger than we are now.

Perhaps the most important concern of a new firm is to get jobs. How did you go about promoting yourselves?

It's important to let people know that you exist. However, in our case, we each had individual reputations, so we had to establish the fact that we were a studio. Once we did that we hoped clients would trust us to take on more substantive assignments. That was one thing that had to be stressed in a promotion piece. The other was the kind of work that we were going to do, and that was somewhat risky because we were committing ourselves to a conceptual style.

The promotion piece we did was called *Great Beginnings.* It was a total package of design and editorial, being a collection of beginnings of famous novels. It showed our typographic skills in exactly the way we hoped to practice them for real clients. It won a lot of awards and became a sought-after keepsake. Most importantly, the work we got from the book was from those clients who wanted the kind of work we proposed. And because it was a sophisticated promotion, clients dealt with us as sophisticated designers. Hence, in our first year we didn't do anything that we would call a bad job.

Coming up with the concept is one thing, but you still had to get supporters: you needed paper, typesetting, and printing. How did that come about?

We got everyone to donate services, except for typesetting. In return we gave all the suppliers credit in the piece. Now, one of the reasons we could do this was because we weren't coming into this cold. We weren't right out of school; we had a certain credibility. The suppliers knew that we

125

would design a good piece and that it was to their advantage to be associated with it in order to promote themselves. People just starting out could try the same route, but it will be hard at first.

Now that you are familiar with running a studio and having a corporate job, how would you compare and contrast them?

I had the best corporate job in the world at Columbia Records. In fact, I could have stayed indefinitely, assuming the quality of the work was high, because the perks and other advantages were so great. If one is worried about security and wants a regular salary check, a clean desk, and a secretary, then the corporation is a terrific place. You don't have to worry about your phone bill and you get an expense account. It's a comfortable life. The problem is, as someone explained to me a long time ago, that when you work for a corporation you only have one client, and if the client goes under or changes politically or decides for whatever reason it doesn't want to deal with you, then you have nothing. On the other hand, if you work for your own firm, then if one client goes, you have others. Of course, owning your own company requires much more responsibility and accounting, but now I am prepared to accept the ebbs and flows of this business.

It took me two years to overcome my insecurity. I had to be weaned from the corporate life. And I don't advise it for everybody.

Well, that leads us to ask what advice you might give to those who are determined to give it a try.

There are two ways to start. One is to do it when you are young, so you become accustomed to the life-style, or, two, do it when you are very well established and everybody knows you. The fact is that I started my business when I was thirty-five years old and I was not ready to be poor. I had to make some severe cuts in my life-style because I had to throw all my finances into the business. It was a huge risk, and I'm glad I took it.

Would you encourage students to get a good job before going into private business?

A student just out of school should be trading man-hours for experience. Get a low-paying job in a good studio or prestigious company for a little while. It's a mutually exploitative situation, but having a good name on a résumé is worth a lot of cash in the long run. That's the nature of the business. There's nothing democratic about graphic design.

You have spoken about school and about business. What about a component that has nothing to do with creativity—networking?

There is a social part of the business that's very important. People should go to openings and involve themselves in the design community so they can meet other people and develop relationships. And it's all right as long as you've got something to contribute. There are people who do nothing but self-promote, and because their work is terrible, they try to make up for it by being gadflies. Watch out, because that can become very irritating to others. So it comes down to a question of behavior. I don't know how to advise doing it well. I don't know that anybody really does it well. It's just a matter of knowing how to make yourself visible without being obnoxious.

FRAN SEIGEL is an artists' representative working in New York City.

What do you look for when deciding whether or not to represent a young or established illustrator?

127

At this time my business is becoming more and more focused on a large number of services to a small number of artists. I prefer that my group stay small, somewhere around four. I look for three things in terms of overall approach. One is style. The style cannot be competitive with my other talent and must be something that I'm very strongly attracted to and feel that I can sell. The second is availability, which translates into a close partnership or exclusive relationship. And the third is a certain degree of rapport and enthusiasm that is really obvious between us. I think that's based on business and personal values.

What are the qualities that you think will sell?

I have certain areas where I have developed strong contacts, including conceptually oriented magazine illustration, book jackets, and most advertising areas. I'm also involved in packaging. I handle a wide market, but not every artist is wide-market-oriented. I do not handle much straightforward or "narrative" realism, fashion artists, or children's book illustration, although many other representatives do. I prefer to represent artists who can work well in most areas where I already have strong affinities and contacts.

At present you handle illustrators only. What would you say is the difference between representing a designer versus an illustrator?

A designer handles the overall layout and graphic approach of a project, or, in short, has different responsibilities than someone who basically handles the pictorial side. Two of my illustrators do some hand-lettering, but it's not a major concern. A designer is involved with areas that are not my strong suits. That's why I don't handle them, not because their work is not of interest to me.

What do you think is the most effective way to promote the artists you handle?

I think promotion encompasses a broad range of things, not only printed materials, but showing the artist to clients in the best light. I encourage entering all types of juried shows, but paid advertising in the directories—I've done very well with *American Showcase*—is my most successful promotion. It is much better than the mailing cards, which I did for three years and which did not get nearly as much work. We have also received many calls from the *American Illustration* annual. I work very closely with the artist to plan the right promotion and promotion vehicles. Where the work is placed, what samples are shown, and how they are presented all have a major impact on what jobs we will be called to do.

Do you work equally as hard on arranging the right portfolio? If so, do you have any pointers?

I work very closely with my artists on *everything* that affects their image, and a portfolio is absolutely number one. It is crucial to show the right things to the right people, and we won't show the same portfolio to different clients. I have various combinations of laminated pieces and transparencies that are exactly the same size, so that they can be interchanged and geared specifically to the markets we are aiming for.

You have prescribed needs and a limited stable, but how would you recommend that someone go about finding a representative?

Anyone who is looking for a rep would be best off talking to ten or fifteen, if the interviews can be arranged. Everyone has a different point of view, varying tastes, and unique procedures. Some work on an informal handshake or a broker arrangement.

Some handle large numbers. Some will work only in specific geographical areas. In any case, it's going to be either a major opportunity or it could be a mistake, so the research is very important.

One interesting note is that it's almost becoming a buyer's market for reps at this point: I get about ten or twelve envelopes and phone calls per week from artists. Also, I believe that most artists will benefit from representing themselves—at least for a year or two—before deciding that they want to work with a representative.

What are the general business arrangements between an artist and agent?

Most reps work on about 25 percent commission. Sometimes the artists may handle a few previous clients on their own, but if it is an exclusive relationship, then most or all of the clients will be included. There may be situations where a rep will work with an artist for lower percentages on previously established accounts. There may be higher percentages when a rep has an out-of-town artist, which is very frequent. So I would say that it would depend on the specific representative. It's always negotiable, and one cannot expect rep A to give the same figures as reps B or C, because the services may be very different.

Most illustrators' reps handle the billing. I think that we bill the job better because we have negotiated the exact terms of the agreement, and that way it's not secondhand.

Do you have any tips on billing for the artist who does not care to have a rep?

Everything concerning work and money should be very clear up front. For example, most clients will cover shipping charges, and many will cover photography charges if something needs to be photographed for reference on a job. Regardless, everything that is billable should be spoken about and clarified before the job is even initiated. Except for magazine work, I get a purchase order on every job before starting. It's very dangerous not to have this document, because without it you don't have proof of what rights have been agreed to and whether the art is to be returned. It also affects sales taxes and other things that the artist or the representative may be required to collect from the client.

RITASUE SIEGEL is the president of RitaSue Siegel Agency Inc. and Design Executive Search.

What services do you provide and for whom?

We recruit designers for companies, consultants, and institutions. We have two companies: RitaSue Siegel Agency is a contingency company, which means we don't get paid until we fill the job. The other is called Design Executive Search, which recruits design managers, partners, or other very experienced people on a search basis, meaning we are paid to complete the assignment on the assumption that we will be successful. We search for designers—we don't wait for them to call us. We recruit graphic, interior, product, and exhibit designers, as well as architects, illustrators, related sales and marketing people, and the support people: drafters, graphic arts production people, modelers, and so on.

Do you interview graduating students or entry-level professionals?

It seems like almost every recent grad calls us. We usually ask them to drop off their portfolios, if they are locals, and we look at the portfolios every day. The only recent grads who get appointments without dropoffs are those who have been recommended to us by their teachers or by a client of ours whose opinion we trust. It would be physically impossible to interview everyone who calls.

Do you give forthright critiques of the portfolios?

Not without an interview. When we can't help someone, our incoming information coordinator will usually just say so. Sometimes she will give general advice based on the comments we've made when looking at the portfolio.

What happens when people are given appointments?

Then they come in with a résumé and portfolio. We ask what they are interested in and what their best suit is. This doesn't mean we want them to be locked into a specific thing, like food packaging, but it helps us if they have a general idea about an area they'd like to learn more about. Of course, if they want to do something very specific, like package design or corporate identity, they should have examples of this type of work. We find that recent grads' goals range from "I'll try anything" to something very specific. Many of them do not have samples related to their interests, and we suggest that they make them. They also need to have design concept sketches to show how they arrived at a solution. Recent grads, for as long as I can remember, always try to have everything in their portfolios perfectly finished or printed. But our best clients always want to see how they think and how they would communicate design concepts in a real situation. So those concept sketches are very important.

Do you have freelance as well as full-time designers?

Yes, but we do not have beginning freelancers. We feel it's important to know that our freelance people are going to deliver, which is only possible given a track record. Also, if someone calls us for a freelancer, they want a pro who can deliver on time and requires no monitoring. The majority of the assignments we handle are for full-timers with experience. Seventy-five percent of the job openings we have are in parts of the country other than New York. We also offer positions outside the U.S., but generally for foreign clients.

What about the young professional, someone who has had either a few freelance jobs or a regular job and then wants to use your service?

Most of the requests we have from clients are for people with two to three years' experience up to design managers in companies and "heavyweight" design directors in consulting groups. We are always looking for people with design excellence and project management ability.

Candidates call and speak to our incoming information coordinator, who asks questions such as, Where are you working? What are your responsibilities? Why do you want to change jobs? What are you looking for in a new job? What are your location preferences? and, What do you want to earn? Persons who work for one of our clients automatically get an appointment, because our philosophy is if they are good enough for our clients, they're probably going to be good enough for us. Otherwise, the "intake form," which contains the answers to the questions, is passed to the people who do the interviewing. We do a lot of screening through the mail. We ask them to send us twenty 35-millimeter slides of their best work and a typed description of the projects. We then make up what we call a skill sheet, which indicates all the vital information regarding salary and goals. It also includes our opinion of the individual and the work. All this material is passed on to the client.

Do you encourage students or young professionals to go into any specific areas?

Not really, although we do discuss what we know about the areas to be sure they have a realistic picture. We encourage people to go into an area that seems appropriate to their talents and interests. We have no favorite areas. We do not see people who want to make a career in advertising, only because we do not get those assignments.

I went to a conference last spring at the Philadelphia College of Art, which was sponsored by the Design Management Seminars. People from industry, education, and consulting firms told each other what their expectations and problems were. I repeated a story that Massimo Vignelli [the New York-based designer] told about students in Italy who were trained as technicians—production people, who had more success as designers than any design school graduates did. He was commenting on the lack of technical training that design students get, and it reminded me that there are marvelous careers to be had in production and studio management that most design students know nothing about. Not everyone is a genius designer, but there is lots of money to be made in production because there are so few capable people in this area. There are some grads who will never make more than $20,000 a year as a designer, but might be able to make as much as $75,000 as head of print production for a major agency. Our clients are always looking for such people.

ELAINE SOREL is a consultant who, through seminars and private sessions, works exclusively on career-development problems of artists and designers.

As a "business therapist" you are really doing something very unique for the designer and illustrator. Can you describe the process?

I am a therapist in the sense that healing is part of what I do. I don't want anybody to get this mixed up with psychotherapy. I work to change bad habits and attitudes within the professional sphere without determining why they exist or where they come from. I'm working with people in the field to over-

come procrastination and fear of success. I'm help-
ing them in terms of presentation, promotion, and
marketing techniques to build long-term professional relationships and to overcome the notion that
the client is the enemy, which many artists feel.
My overall goal is to increase awareness of professional performance and uniqueness. I want to help
identify what it is that they do best, so that together
we can create a strategy to use that work in the
professional world. I would like artists to be com-
pensated for the work they love to do and to be accepted by their peers. I've summed it up for people
by saying that I can help creative people to become
creative business people and to feel that by selling
their work they are not selling out.

Do you work with designers or illustrators?

I work with all disciplines: illustrators, art directors, photographers, and writers.

Do you help people find jobs?

I don't give clients names of people to see, because
I am not a placement agency. I help people develop their career. What I offer is not designed for
the short term, but for the long haul.

How much do you charge for a consultation?

I charge $80 an hour and I generally recommend
two hours for an initial consultation. Sometimes
that's all that's needed.

What advice do you offer to young artists?

I suggest that they follow what interests them. If
they feel passionate about illustration, that's what
they should pursue. I get people in touch with what
they feel best about doing and encourage them not
to censor it because they think that it's not commercial. I think good money comes with doing what
you love to do.

People starting out must identify what will give them the most pleasure and then be unrelenting and patient in the pursuit of it. And, finally, promote yourself like crazy. Make yourself as visible as possible by doing whatever you can afford to do. The key here is to dare to be different; dare to be bold. Don't assume that what you see published has to be what you should show.

Often, beginners are anxious about making calls and showing their portfolios. They feel that they should wait for the anxiety to stop before they make the rounds. My feeling is to think of the anxiety itself as a divine energy. Don't wait for it to go away. Anxiety goes away in *doing* what is difficult. Use it to move forward.

PAMELA VASSIL is art director for special features of the *New York Daily News*. She also teaches a course in pasteup, mechanicals, and illustration at Parsons School of Design in New York City.

You see many professional portfolios, and you have advised your students as to the most effective means of presenting work. What goals do you set for the good illustration portfolio?

It should seduce the art director.

That's to the point. What will seduce you?

There are some art directors who get confused if there are too many styles in a book. They say silly things like, "I can't tell what you do." Well, the truth of the matter is that an individual can do a lot of stuff, and I like to see that diversity in a portfolio. In addition to that, I look for good drawing, and then good ideas, and finally a sense of humor.

Many art directors are reluctant to give forthright critiques of portfolios. Do you, as a rule, give an honest assessment of the work you see?

It depends. If an artist is ripping someone else off, then I will say something like, "If I wanted Brad Holland, I'd call him." If the artist's talent is basically sound, I'll say that I don't think it's the proper direction to go in and that he or she could probably make it better with a more personal style. If the illustrator is really awful—I mean *really* awful—what can you say? The simplest thing is "thank you very much."

Do you have any formal requirements for a portfolio?

I think there should be some sort of logical pacing, so that all the color or all the black-and-white is not lumped together. It should be interspersed to show range and, moreover, be surprising. I don't care much whether the work is ensleeved or laminated. Obviously, if a portfolio is really sleek, it will look very impressive on the surface, but I've had people come to see me with great work that they've taken out of a paper bag.

Like so many art directors, I have a very tight schedule and limited time to see illustrators, so I ask them to initially drop off their books. I cannot stand humongous portfolios; you know, those big things that look like pizza boxes.

Do you like to see work in any particular stages of development?

Unless there is an entire process showing a job from start to finish, I don't much care whether or not they show a sketch in the midst of their finishes. I prefer, when possible, to meet with the illustrator and talk, because that's the only way to know if the work was their idea or an art director's idea.

Do you think it matters how an illustrator acts or looks?

Yes and no. If somebody looks like they just walked off of Times Square, I might be a little put off. But, basically, the work really speaks for itself. I think art directors are more tolerant than editors, though. If an illustrator has to meet with an editor, pulling oneself together simply suggests a responsible nature.

You receive scores of mailers each month. Do you respond to them, or do they go directly in the circular file?

I like mailers and keep some of them. I have even called illustrators for work based on certain mailing pieces.

There are a couple of requisites for effective mailers: make two of them, one in color and the other in black-and-white, and make sure the phone number is easy to read. For beginners with limited funds, it's not necessary to do a campaign; just send a mailer out and make follow-up calls (and not three months after the mailing either).

There are some illustrators from whom I get a mailing once a week. At some point I get annoyed because they know that if I had a job for them I would have called already. I feel assaulted and, ultimately, they are wasting a lot of money.

Apart from the portfolio and the mailer, what do you think a young illustrator must do or know to get work?

For anyone beginning there must be an emphasis upon the word. For the editorial illustrator this is the only way to deal with an editor on his linear terms. There are so many artists from all across the country trying to get the good jobs in New York that one has to have an edge on the next person, which, in my opinion, is something verbal. In being able to express oneself there is strength.

FOR YOUR REFERENCE

PART THREE

1.
DEVELOPING A GRAPHIC ARTS LIBRARY

Whether you are an illustrator or a designer, a free-lancer or a full-time employee, it is a necessity, not a luxury, to have a well-stocked graphic arts library (or at least ready access to one). A library is a source of technical information and scrap material. Moreover, everyone should know at least a little about the history of design, illustration, and related fields, if for no other reason than to avoid reinventing the wheel. Hundreds of histories, in and out of print, cover art and design movements and styles. However, because one's funds are limited at the outset of a career, the most essential books are those that will serve one's immediate reference needs. These run the gamut from "swipe" or "pick-up" books (including the low-cost reprints of old advertising books that Dover has been publishing for decades) to art directors' and illustrators' annuals (which, by showing the "best" work of the year, provide an extensive influence file). They also include everything from the scores of coffee table books on subjects ranging from animals to zeppelins to common type-specimen books. One should also collect as many art supply and paper company catalogs as possible.

Although most large public library systems offer free picture file services, and some cities, such as New York and Los Angeles, have various stock houses and private picture collections that charge fees, these are not substitutes for a private reference collection when it comes to saving time and money.

The bibliography at the end of this book offers some suggestions for histories, swipe books, and technical manuals. But the best way to find and familiarize yourself with the large number of titles is to spend some time in bookshops. In addition to browsing in large stores like Waldenbooks or B. Dalton (which, for the most part, carry only new books), you should frequent secondhand and remainder bookstores, which will provide you with terrific material at cut-rate prices. Book fairs and public library sales are also founts of reasonably priced, usually out-of-print, material.

Sadly, many stores do not sell design- or illustration-related books, so it may be necessary to join at least one or all of the graphic arts book clubs listed below. These and other mail-order services (including the ones advertised in *Print*, *Art Direction* and *Communication Arts* magazines) offer the most recently published books at a discount.

AMERICAN ARTIST BOOK CLUB
Watson-Guptill Publications
1515 Broadway
New York, N.Y.   10036

Emphasis on painting, drawing, and illustration. Regularly features graphic design titles. No obligation to buy additional books after the initial purchase.

GRAPHIC ARTIST'S BOOK CLUB
P.O. Box 429566
Cincinnati, Ohio   45242-9566

For professionals in the graphic arts field. Emphasis on stimulating creative growth and productivity. Also a selection of the newest and most important books available from around the world.

NORTH LIGHT BOOK CLUB
9933 Alliance Road
Cincinnati, Ohio   45242

Emphasis on how-to advice regarding every medium and technique. Also, a large selection of art books from around the world.

PRINT MAGAZINE BOOK CLUB
355 Lexington Avenue
New York, N.Y.   10017

Wide selection of graphic design and illustration books and annuals, including histories, monographs, and how-to books.

ANNUALS The most accessible resources for contemporary illustrators and designers are the many annuals published by various design magazines and graphic arts organizations and available either for free or at a discount as a benefit of membership (see Part 3, Chapter 3). While the contents of these books are usually selected by juries (with the idea that consensus determines the best quality), sometimes the selections are quirky. Regardless, annuals are the best record of the preceding year's work. They can be purchased in bookshops, through the appropriate organizations, or from mail-order services or book clubs.

MAGAZINES

In addition to a library of books, a collection of graphic arts magazines is immensely useful, albeit costly. The field is awash with periodicals that specialize in everything from printing news to design history, as well as those that cover the field more generally. At the outset you should subscribe only to those journals whose subjects affect you directly. With this in mind, we recommend the following (please write or call for up-to-date subscription information).

AIGA JOURNAL (quarterly)

American Institute of Graphic Arts
1059 Third Avenue
New York, N.Y.   10021
(212) 752-0813

This publication of the American Institute of Graphic Arts covers and analyzes the issues and events related to graphic design. The *Journal* is available for free if you join the AIGA. Otherwise you can buy it by subscription.

ART DIRECTION (bimonthly)

10 East 39th Street
New York, N.Y.   10016
(212) 889-6500

Noted for its exotic covers, *Art Direction* offers trade news from around the country, including information about positions and personnel, newly breaking campaigns and designs, and the latest graphic trends. Each issue highlights an up-and-coming illustrator and photographer. The magazine also serves as a catalog for a large mail-order book list.

144

COMMUNICATION ARTS (eight issues per year)
410 Sherman Avenue
P.O. Box 10300
Palo Alto, Calif.   94303
(415) 326-6040

Through handsomely and profusely illustrated feature
stories on significant contemporary practitioners, *C.A.*
covers a broad spectrum of concerns, ranging from illustration to corporate, environmental, advertising, and
publication design. Regular columns offer information
on business ethics, printing technology, new and note-
worthy products, recent books, and forthcoming events.
Four of its issues are jury-selected annuals devoted to illustration, photography, design, and advertising.

GRAPHIS (bimonthly)
141 Lexington Avenue
New York, N.Y.   10017

For the past forty-four years this Zurich-based publication has reported intelligently on international design
practitioners and trends in three languages: English,
German, and French. Now under new ownership, a
redesigned *Graphis* continues to showcase international
illustration and design events in four foreign-language
editions—English, German, French, and Japanese.

PRINT (bimonthly)
355 Lexington Avenue
New York, N.Y.   10017
(212) 682-0830

By far the most eclectic of the journals cited thus far,
Print offers informative articles of contemporary and historical interest, from artist/designer profiles to forgotten
magazines. The journal's "mini-portfolios" showcase the
work of new illustrators, designers, and photographers;
its regular features report on technology and products
and offer book reviews and design criticism. Books can
be purchased through order forms in the magazine. An
annual *Regional Design* issue is published every fall.

UPPER AND LOWER CASE (quarterly)
2 Hammarskjold Plaza
New York, N.Y.   10017
(212) 371-0699

Published by the International Typeface Corporation,
this magazine is sent out for free to over one hundred
fifty thousand readers worldwide. While it is in-

tended to showcase ITC's typefaces, it also contains regular features on technology, the history of typography, significant artists, and satiric art. Included as well are typographic games, articles on type-related ephemera, and the "*U&lc* Bookshelf." The advertisements for products and typography are also good sources of information.

The following are recommended as supplements to the journals listed above. Each provides information on a specific aspect of graphic art.

ADWEEK (weekly)
820 Second Avenue
New York, N.Y.   10017
(212) 661-8080

Full of news and information concerning the advertising world. Also publishes a monthly editorial section that features reports on specific areas of the advertising business, including television and radio.

AIRBRUSH DIGEST (bimonthly)
521 S.W. 11th Avenue
Portland, Oreg.   97205-2691

Concerned with the art and technique of airbrush rendering.

AMERICAN ARTIST (bimonthly)
1515 Broadway
New York, N.Y.   10036
(212) 764-7300

Primarily aimed at the professional and amateur painter, watercolorist, and sculptor. Regularly has articles on illustrators and cartoonists. The annual art school issue is an invaluable resource for prospective students.

FINE PRINT (four issues per year)
P.O. Box 3394
San Francisco, Calif.   94119

Devoted to the art of fine typography and the fine press book. Beautifully printed by letterpress and offset, this periodical is as much an aesthetic experience as it is a fount of information and ideas. Included are historical surveys, critical analyses of type, and reviews of relevant books and exhibitions.

146

GRAPHIC DESIGN U.S.A. (bimonthly)
120 East 56th Street
New York, N.Y.   10022
(212) 759-8813

Primarily a record of trade news and information.

HOW (bimonthly)
355 Lexington Avenue
New York, N.Y.   10017
(212) 682-0830

In-depth case histories trace the development of illustration; book, record, and poster design; typography; advertising campaigns; photography; and animation.

ID: MAGAZINE OF INTERNATIONAL DESIGN (bimonthly)
330 West 42d Street
New York, N.Y.   10036
(212) 695-4955

Covers all design disciplines, including graphic, package, industrial, and experimental. Its *Annual Design Review* is an analytical report of the year's significant events in these areas.

MAGAZINE DESIGN AND PRODUCTION (monthly)
4551 West 107th Street, Suite 343
Overland Park, Kans.   66207

One of the most well written and well edited trade magazines aimed at printers and production managers. Interesting angles are explored in articles on commonplace subjects, such as art direction, composition systems, and illustration.

STEP BY STEP GRAPHICS (bimonthly)
6000 N. Forest Park Drive
P.O. Box 1901
Peoria, Ill.   61656
(800) 255-8800

In-depth, step-by-step articles illustrated with full-color examples focus on the hands-on processes of design and illustration.

STUDIO (six issues per year)
215 Carlingview Drive
Rexdale, Ontario
M2J 4V6 Canada
(416) 675-1999

Well-written articles on a broad range of graphic arts, including typography, illustration, and photography. Features on copyrights and computer graphics, as well as a yearly competition, make this the leading design magazine in Canada.

COLLECTING NONPROFESSIONAL MAGAZINES

The well-rounded library should also include current trade and commercial magazines that are both editorially and visually interesting. Such nonprofessional magazines often reflect, and sometimes initiate, design and illustration trends and are therefore sources of good ideas. Of course, thousands of large and small magazines and newspaper magazine supplements are published every year, so simply browse among the periodical shelves of your local library and newsdealer as time permits.

BUILDING A SCRAP FILE

Magazines are also excellent sources of material for a scrap file, or a loosely or systematically organized collection of all forms of visual reference, eclectic or specific. As mentioned, many libraries offer picture or scrap collection services, but your own well-stocked collection will be most accessible. A useful scrap file is cultivated over time, so do not feel you must have it all at once. At first the file may simply be a collection of magazine and newspaper tearings or of loose pages or photographs bought at junk shops and flea markets—anything that you think might come in handy for a future job.

It is best to organize your material in folders or loose-leaf books, according to subject. However, since that obviously takes time, any type of accessible organization system will do. Some practition-

148

ers even keep files on one anothers' work, to keep abreast of and, one hopes, to avoid mimicking a distinctive style.

Traditionally, suppliers of graphic arts products and services, such as type foundries and printers, have produced elaborate and informative examples of their wares. For at least three decades paper companies, in addition to providing samples of their stocks, have hired the best designers and illustrators to create publications that cover various aspects of design—ranging from monographs on master designers to different applications of packaging or posters. One of the most well known and long-running publications was Westvaco's *Inspirations*, a magazine designed by Bradbury Thompson. A consistently laudable ongoing program is Champion Paper's *Inspiration* series, designed by James Miho. Mohawk Paper Mills and Neenah Paper Company have also produced showcase materials; the former has issued lavish monographic portfolios of work by Saul Bass, Wilson McLean, and Ivan Chermayeff, as well as the semiannual journal *Design and Style*. The latter has issued a sketchbook of Alan E. Cober's work and volumes I and II of *Seymour Chwast's Editorial Image*. These publications not only help sell paper, but provide practitioners with excellent models for their own endeavors. The following annotated list offers the names and addresses of companies that contribute regularly to the collective literature.

AMERICAN PAPER INSTITUTE

260 Madison Avenue
New York, N.Y.   10016
(212) 340-0600

Offers publication entitled *The Cover and Text Book*, a generic reference source that deals with areas ranging from technical guidelines to paper specification.

CHAMPION INTERNATIONAL CORPORATION
One Champion Plaza
Stamford, Conn.   06921
(203) 358-7000

Sponsors a graphic arts award for designers who have demonstrated design excellence on Champion paper. Also sends out creative mailings (including Champion's *Inspiration* series) aimed at the design community.

CURTIS PAPER
Division of James River Corporation
Newark, Del.   19711
(800) 441-9292

Offers promotional samples of various papers. Publishes a 31-page sourcebook, *Type*, that designers will find useful for improving their ability to communicate with typographers and printers and for updating their knowledge on the latest developments in typography.

HOWARD PAPER MILLS INC.
115 Columbia Street
P.O. Box 982
Dayton, Ohio   45401
(513) 224-1211

Sends promotional material to the graphic design community for informational and inspirational purposes. Advises how different papers can accent different reproduction needs.

MEAD PAPER
Fine Paper Division
Courthous Plaza Northwest
Dayton, Ohio   45463
(513) 222-6323

Sponsors the Mead Annual Report Show, now in its thirtieth year, and publishes a full-color catalog.

MOHAWK PAPER MILLS
Cohoes, N.Y.   12047
(212) 581-5101

Publishes *Design & Style*, a journal of historical resource and inspiration, as well as portfolios on leading designers and illustrators.

MONADNOCK PAPER MILLS INC.
Bennington, N.H.   03442
(603) 588-3311

Offers promotional posters as well as folder complete
with sample kits of each text and cover paper Monad-
nock produces.

POTLACH CORPORATION
Northwest Paper Division
207 Avenue C
Cloquet, Minn.   55720
(218) 879-2300

Offers two items of interest to designers: a publication
entitled *Paper Perfect*, which is a sampler of five different paper surfaces showing the printing quality of each;
and a corporate publications planner, which includes a
calendar of six client designer phases of a project and a
workbook with form pages for project pagination, estimates, jobsheets, and specifications.

SPECIAL PAPERS INC.
P.O. Box 643
Wilton, Conn.   06897
(203) 834-2884

Sole representatives of fine art and graphic paper (as opposed to printing paper), manufactured by the Arches
and Canson mills in France. Offers samples of a wide
variety of papers.

S. D. WARREN COMPANY
Division of Scott Paper Company
225 Franklin Street
Boston, Mass.   02101
(617) 423-7300

Provides a free service to designers called the Idea Exchange Library of Printed Samples, which contains over
ten thousand printed samples cross-filed under more
than one hundred industry and graphic categories. A
useful source of printing, design, copy, and promotional
ideas.

2.
RESOURCE AND PROMOTIONAL BOOKS

In recent years promotional books have sprung up in major cities in the United States and Canada. They provide art directors and other clients with access to illustrators, designers, photographers, letterers, and other applied artists. Advertisers in these books (either the individual practitioner or his or her agent) usually buy at least one full-color page to show samples of the artist's work. The following is an annotated list of some of the most successful publications.

ADWEEK ART DIRECTORS INDEX
820 Second Avenue
New York, N.Y.   10017
(212) 661-8080

Portfolio of American creative talent in black-and-white and color.

Categories: Illustration; design; photography.
Distribution: Forty-five thousand total, to ad agencies, corporations, publishers, and major design firms, 15,000 of which are distributed free in the United States. Paid distribution in the United States is 11,000; 19,000 internationally.
Fees: Full-page color $3,250; black-and-white $2,500.
Special Features: Twenty-five hundred free reprints; access to mailing lists of over 15,000 buying contacts; self-promotion presentations to illustrators throughout the country.

ADWEEK PORTFOLIOS
820 Second Avenue
New York, N.Y.   10017
(212) 661-8080

Incorporates the Art Directors Index (see next chapter). Comprehensive directory of creative services.

Categories: Design; illustration; photography; and commercial production (each category constituting a separate portfolio).
Distribution: Twenty thousand circulated free to creative directors, art directors, art buyers, agency producers, and art, design, and advertising executives at client companies. Also sold in bookstores worldwide.
Fees: Listing in regional service directory is free. Additional listings cost from $25 to $3,250.

AMERICAN ILLUSTRATION SHOWCASE

724 Fifth Avenue
New York, N.Y.   10019
(212) 245-0981

Creative directory in black-and-white and color.

Categories: Illustration; representatives; graphic design organizations.
Distribution: Forty thousand worldwide, with free distribution of 16,000 in the United States and 1,500 in Europe and Canada.
Fees: Full-page color $2,350; black-and-white $2,050.
Special Features: Two thousand free reprints.

ARIZONA PORTFOLIO

815 North First Avenue, Suite 1
Phoenix, Ariz.   85003
(602) 252-2332

Directory of all services connected with communication arts. Black-and-white and color.

Categories: Advertising; graphic design; illustration; photography; video production; printing; typography.
Distribution: Ten thousand in nine states: Arizona, California, Colorado, Nevada, New Mexico, Oregon, Texas, Washington, and Utah. Five hundred copies distributed in other major centers in the Midwest and East.
Fees: Full-page color $1,500.

CHICAGO TALENT SOURCEBOOK

212 West Superior, Suite 400
Chicago, Ill.   60610
(312) 944-5115

Complete reference guide to Chicago area creative talent and graphic services. Black-and-white and color.

Categories: Over fifty different categories, including illustration/retouching/reps; design/keyline; and advertising agencies/media.
Distribution: Ten thousand, with 80 percent distributed to local and national art and production buyers.
Fees: Full-page color $1,850; black-and-white $1,400.
Special Features: One thousand free reprints.

CORPORATE SHOWCASE
724 Fifth Avenue
New York, N.Y.   10019
(212) 245-0981

Creative directory in black-and-white and color.

Categories: Illustrators; designers; photographers.
Distribution: Seventeen thousand worldwide, with free
distribution of 10,000 in the United States and 7,000 in
Europe and Canada.
Fees: Full-page color $3,000; black-and-white $2,500.
Special Features: Two thousand free reprints.

CREATIVE BLACK BOOK
401 Park Avenue South
New York, N.Y.   10016
(212) 684-4255

Advertising directory that lists names, addresses, and
phone numbers of artists, designers, and photographers.
Black-and-white and color.

Categories: Supplies and equipment; prints, chromes,
and retouchers; typography/printers, engravers/paper;
design, illustration, creative services; models/talent,
stylists, props, backdrops; television production/post-
production; music, sound, radio, recording studios;
advertising agencies/organizations.
Distribution: United States 10,450; overseas 9,350;
worldwide 40,000. Free distribution of 20,000; circulation includes art directors in more than 7,500 large corporations. Also sent to advertising agencies,
corporations, and publishers.
Fees: Full-page color $5,000; black-and-white $3,600;
double-page color $9,950; double-page black-and-white
$6,500.
Special Features: Free listings are available by sending
your name and address on a letterhead. Two thousand
reprints free with color ads if first mechanical deadline
is met. If not, cost is $400. Will help with marketing
plan, mailers, developing mailing lists, and portfolio
analysis. Offers seminars on how to market yourself.

THE DESIGN DIRECTORY
Wefler & Associates Inc.
2 N. Riverside Plaza
Chicago, Ill.   60606
(312) 454-1940

Directory of firms and consultants in industrial, graphic, and interior design.

Categories: Over 4,000 entries include addresses, telephone numbers, year firms established, number of full-time employees, names and titles of key people, and areas of specialization. Some firms also include their list of clients.

DESIGN SOURCE
Turnbull & Co.
19 Mount Auburn Street
Cambridge, Mass.   02138
(617) 864-1110

Creative talent directory of companies and individuals in New England. Black-and-white and color.

Categories: Design; copywriters, illustration; photography; products/services; typography; printing/finishing; film/video.
Distribution: Ten thousand annually. Eighty-five percent free to buyers of creative services and products in New England, advertising agencies, design firms (47 percent of which distributed to firms in New York City). Fifteen percent sold throughout New England.
Fees: Full-page color $1,460; black-and-white $1,270.
Special Features: One thousand reprints free to buyers of one-half page or larger.

DIRECTORY OF WASHINGTON CREATIVE SERVICES
1506 Nineteenth Street, N.W.
Washington, D.C.   20036
(202) 462-6110

Directory of creative services in Washington metropolitan area, including parts of Baltimore and Richmond. Mainly black-and-white, with some color.

Categories: Advertising/marketing/public relations; audiovisual/film/video; broadcast and print media; editorial and writing; graphics, photographics; suppliers.
Distribution: Free to major advertising agencies in the Washington, Baltimore, and Richmond areas. Paid circulation includes trade associations; government agen-

cies, institutions, and foundations; major corporations; studios; and newspapers.

Fees: Full-page color $1,150; black-and-white $750.

HOUSTON'S GRAPHIC HANDBOOK

c/o Creative Ventures
P.O. Box 27323
Houston, Tex.   77323
(713) 666-1392

Directory of illustrators, designers, and photographers in greater Houston metropolitan area. Black-and-white and color.

Categories: Advertising, artists; graphic support services; film and audiovisual; photography; printing and typography; sound.
Distribution: Three thousand annually. Reaches all areas of graphic communications, advertising, public relations, and marketing directors of corporations. Also sold in book stores.
Fees: Full-page color $700; black-and-white $300.

MADISON AVENUE HANDBOOK

Peter Glenn Publications
17 East 48th Street
New York, N.Y.   10017
(212) 688-7940; (800) 223-1254

Advertising and communications trade directory of talent, service, and suppliers. Black-and-white and color.

Categories: Illustration, design, printing/allied services, props services, film commissions/locations; animation/special effects; film; video; agencies; media.
Distribution: Twenty-five thousand copies printed; free to all advertisers.
Fees: Full-page color $3,000; black-and-white $1,950.
Special Features: Five hundred free reprints to color advertisers.

RSVP

P.O. Box 314
Brooklyn, N.Y.   11205
(718) 857-9267

Directory of creative talent. Black-and-white and color.

Categories: Illustration; design; photography; technical services.
Distribution: Twelve thousand total, with over 7,000 sent to advertising agencies, publishers, and corporations na-

tionwide. Also sold at art supply and book stores
throughout the United States and Canada.
Fees: Full-page color $1,150; black-and-white $795.
Special Features: One thousand reprints $200; twenty-
four-hour callback answering service; annual illustration
competition for college seniors, with cash prizes
awarded and all finalist work included in a special section of the directory.

SOUTH EAST CREATIVE DIRECTORY
802 Stovall Boulevard, N.E.
Atlanta, Ga.   30342
(404) 261-7599

Directory that lists creative services in the following
states alphabetically within each section: Alabama,
Florida, Georgia, Kentucky, Louisiana, Mississippi,
North Carolina, South Carolina, Tennessee, and Virginia. Black-and-white and color.

Categories: Illustration; photography; suppliers; audiovisual; production; sound and music; postproduction;
equipment; talent and media.
Distribution: Eight thousand regionally and nationally.
Sent to every advertising agency billing over one million
dollars in a ten-state area and to every agency billing
over five million dollars nationwide.
Fees: Full-page color $1,300; black-and-white $950.

3. PROFESSIONAL CLUBS AND ASSOCIATIONS

Belonging to graphic design organizations keeps you in touch with the community. Local organizations, such as art directors', illustrators', and advertising clubs, as well as AIGA chapters, allow you to meet colleagues and suppliers and keep you informed about the design events in your locale. National organizations offer a means to meet and exchange ideas with professionals on a broader scale. Additional advantages to membership are annuals, newsletters, and opportunities to enter competitions, as well as group insurance and discounts on supplies. The following is an annotated list of some of the most significant organizations nationwide.

ADVERTISING CLUB OF NEW YORK

155 East 55th Street, Suite 202
New York, N.Y.   10022
(212) 935-8080

Founded 1906 to bring together persons interested in advertising, marketing, and related fields.

Educational Programs: Sixteen-lecture advertising and marketing course; advanced advertising minicourses.
Awards: Annual Andy Awards saluting creative and communication excellence.
Publication: AdNews (newsletter).

ADVERTISING FEDERATION OF MINNESOTA

416 East Hennepin Avenue
Minneapolis, Minn.   55414
(612) 379-1645

Nonprofit professional organization of people within the advertising industry.

Educational Programs: Student internship/scholarship programs; seminars for small-business owners.
Competition/Exhibition: The Show, annual event co-sponsored by the Art Directors/Copywriters Club of Minnesota. Winning entries granted awards and featured in *AFM* annual.
Conference: Business communications forum held each May.
Publications: The Show (annual); *Format* (quarterly magazine).

AMERICAN COUNCIL FOR THE ARTS

570 Seventh Avenue
New York, N.Y.   10018
(212) 354-6655

Founded 1960. Dedicated to supporting the arts in
America and to shaping cultural policy, the Council
seeks to achieve a healthier arts environment both for
artists and the general public. Representatives work regularly with congressional leaders and other key policy-
makers to ensure that the arts are strongly supported in
Washington.

Member Benefits: Discounts from ACA Books, a nonprofit publisher and distributor of books on the arts;
group health insurance.
Publication: ACA Update (monthly newsletter that sum-
marizes trends on the national art scene).

AMERICAN ILLUSTRATION, INC.

67 Irving Place
New York, N.Y.   10003
(212) 460-5558

Focuses on current trends in illustration.

Educational Program: Graphic Arts Weekend, featuring
lectures, conferences, and studio visits, held each fall.
Competition/Exhibition: Annual juried competition for
students and professionals (certificates awarded).
Publication: American Illustration (annual).

AMERICAN INSTITUTE OF GRAPHIC ARTS

1059 Third Avenue
New York, N.Y.   10021
(212) 752-0813

Founded 1914. A national nonprofit organization of
graphic arts professionals that represents the interests of
the graphic design community. Conducts an interrelated
program of competitions, exhibitions, publications, educational activities, and public interest projects to promote excellence in and advancement of the field.
Established a code of ethics and professional conduct.
Compiled and published a listing of archival source materials on the history of graphic design, and an international list of contemporary periodicals related to the
field. Members are involved in the design and production of books, magazines, and periodicals, as well as
corporate, environmental, and promotional graphics.
Chapters have been formed in Boston, Cleveland, Los

Angeles, New York, Philadelphia, San Francisco, Texas, and Washington, D.C.

Member Benefits: Slide archive of exhibitions over the past six years, which may be rented for lectures and seminars; group insurance; library and archival resource.
Educational Programs: Lectures; seminars.
Competitions/Exhibitions: Annual book show featuring book designs; annual communication graphics show featuring reports, logos, stationery, promotional materials, and corporate graphics; biannual cover show featuring record albums, magazine covers, book jackets, and annual report covers; "mental picture" show focusing on changing illustration themes; annual exhibitions on file at Columbia University's Low Library and at the Library of Congress.
Conference: Held biannually.
Publications: AIGA Journal of Graphic Design (quarterly newsletter); *AIGA Graphic Design USA* (annual); membership directory (distributed free); education directory listing over 280 institutions.

ART DIRECTORS & ARTISTS CLUB OF SACRAMENTO
2791 24th Street
Sacramento, Calif.   95818
(916) 731-8802

Founded 1966. Focuses on educational programs within the design field.

Member Benefits: Legal services; credit union; financial counseling; discounts at local art stores; insurance programs; information about job openings; "survival kit" (see under Publications).
Educational Programs: Business by Design, a two-day conference for professionals that focuses on the business issues of a design career; Envision, a two-day conference held each spring that features workshops, guest speakers, and a student poster competition, the winner of which receives a $500 scholarship; monthly lecture series with guest speakers.
Competition/Exhibition: Student poster event (see under Educational Programs).
Publications: Etcetera (quarterly newsletter, with annual commemorative edition); Survival Kit containing organizational charts, legal forms, and information about production control for new members.

ART DIRECTORS CLUB

250 Park Avenue South
New York, N.Y.   10003
(212) 674-0500

Founded 1920. A trade organization for graphic arts
professionals, ADC is a major exhibitor of advertising,
editorial, and television art and design; a social club
and meeting place; a promoter of art education; and a
center for information on industry issues and individual
problems, which services professionals, art students and
faculties, government agencies, and corporations. Offers
an expanding educational program that seeks, among
other goals, to aid students coming into the field. Members advise schools and students on professional issues
and help staff to answer letters on questions relating to
art education and careers.

Member Benefits: Free copy of the *Art Directors Annual*;
use of club library; job placement.
Educational Programs: Scholarships for needy, talented
young people; portfolio review for graduating students;
luncheon and evening speaker programs.
Competitions/Exhibitions: Annual competition, with
awards granted to winning entries; gallery exhibits.
Publications: Art Directors Club bimonthly newsletter;
Art Directors Annual.

ART DIRECTORS CLUB OF LOS ANGELES

5000 Van Nuys Boulevard, Suite 400
Sherman Oaks, Calif.   91403
(818) 995-7339

Founded 1948 to satisfy a need among communication
arts specialists to share experiences and information
with peers.

Educational Programs: Monthly lectures by guest speakers on all areas of art direction and graphic arts.
Awards: The Best in the West Awards given in more
than forty categories of art direction and graphic design.
Publication: Newsletter.

ART DIRECTORS CLUB OF METROPOLITAN WASHINGTON

655 15th Street N.W., Suite 300
Washington, D.C.   20005
(202) 639-4600

Founded 1953. Education is a major interest of the
club, which sponsors many seminars and forums for
students.

Member Benefit: Fraternal Aid Committee reviews portfolios and résumés from artists, designers, and art directors looking for full- or part-time work in the area.
Educational Programs: Scholarship fund providing financial help for talented art students in the area; Career Day sponsored yearly by the Education Committee, which gives students the opportunity to present their portfolios to top art directors in the community; seminars; lectures.
Competitions/Exhibitions: Annual Art Directors Exhibit granting awards to and showcasing the best of advertising, editorial, and graphic design on the East Coast; the Real Show, an event that gives students problems to solve and awards winners in each of a variety of categories with scholarships and an exhibition of their work.
Publications: Annual of winning entries from the Real Show; *Fullbleed* (newsletter).

ARTISTS GUILD OF CHICAGO

664 North Michigan Avenue, Suite 720
Chicago, Ill.   60611
(312) 951-8252

Founded 1902. Professional organization of art directors, illustrators, designers, photographers, fine artists, and production artists.

Educational Programs: Sketch trips; studio tours; public service projects, including fundraising for scholarships in art schools.
Exhibition: Produced by members.
Publication: Pegasus (monthly newsletter).

ARTISTS IN PRINT

Building D, Fort Mason Center
San Francisco, Calif.   94123
(415) 673-6941

Founded 1974 to enhance the exchange of skills, information, and ideas among Bay Area graphic artists.

Member Benefits: Access to job file providing information about the needs of the business community; use of graphics library and resource center; medical and dental insurance.
Educational Program: Workshops with top people in the field.
Publication: Graphiti (newsletter).

THE CANADA COUNCIL
255 Albert Street
P.O. Box 1047
Ottawa, Ontario
K1P 5U8 Canada
(613) 237-3400

Founded 1957 to promote arts in Canada. Provides
3,700 grants each year to professional Canadian artists
and arts organizations.

Awards: Canada Council Children's Literature Prizes
(four awards of $5,000 each) given to Canadian writers
and illustrators of books for young people, who have
published in Canada or abroad during the preceding calendar year.

CANADIAN ASSOCIATION OF PHOTOGRAPHERS
AND ILLUSTRATORS IN COMMUNICATIONS
69 Sherbourne, Suite 222
Toronto, Ontario
M5A 3X7 Canada
(416) 364-1223; 364-1224

Founded 1976 to safeguard and promote the interests of
photographers and illustrators in the communications industry and to maintain high professional standards and
ethics. The Archives and Awards Committee is responsible for archival research and storage of information pertaining to the history of Canadian illustration and
photography.

Member Benefit: Insurance.
Educational Programs: Portfolio nights enabling members to meet and view the work of well-known professionals; business-practice seminars.
Competition/Exhibition: Annual jury-selected exhibition
of members' work.
Awards: Development of program honoring professional
achievements.
Publication: Vision (quarterly newsletter).

CARTOONISTS ASSOCIATION
Box 4203 Grand Central Station
New York, N.Y.   10017
(212) 677-3317

Founded 1980. Professional association of creative artists, predominantly freelance, who are interested in
maintaining high standards and establishing better business relations between buyers and sellers of magazine

cartoons. Provides cartoonists with information about markets, opportunities, and rates, and provides buyers, in turn, with information about cartoonists. Members must be professional cartoonists, preferably in the magazine field, and must submit eight samples for board approval.

Conference: Semi-annual business meetings for members.
Exhibition: Held annually at Master Eagle Gallery, New York City.

CARTOONISTS GUILD
30 East 20th Street
New York, N.Y.   10003
(212) 777-7353

Founded 1967. Division of the Graphic Artists Guild.

Member Benefits: Automatic membership in the Graphic Artists Guild; *Marketing Opportunity Bulletin*, which lists magazine fees, schedules, and terms.
Conferences: Monthly meetings; annual convention in New York City.
Publications: Cartoonews (monthly newsletter); *Cartoonists Guild Brief*, offering news of the industry. (See also under Member Benefits.)

CENTER FOR ARTS INFORMATION
625 Broadway
New York, N.Y.   10012
(212) 677-7548

Founded 1976. Cross-disciplinary information and management assistance center. Reference and referral services available to all members of the arts profession, as well as to the general public. Staff responds to a wide range of questions posed by arts organizations, individual artists, and sponsors. Equipped with a library of over sixty thousand reference books, pamphlets, and directories and more than 325 arts periodicals. Maintains files on service organizations and funding agencies, and brochures on current workshops, seminars, and conferences.

Publication: For Your Information (quarterly newsletter).

COLLEGE ART ASSOCIATION OF AMERICA
149 Madison Avenue
New York, N.Y.   10016
(212) 889-2113

Founded 1911. National organization created to encourage excellence both in the teaching and practice of art and art history. Members include critics, scholars, teachers, artists, museum professionals, art dealers and collectors, and art and slide librarians. Canvases 1,600 colleges, museums, art centers, and publishers for available positions and offers job listings and placement services to members and nonmembers alike. Lists of current openings are compiled and mailed five times annually.

Member Benefits: Group insurance plan; reduced-price subscriptions to art periodicals.
Conference: Annual meeting devoted to papers on art historical research, with sessions on criticism and the arts.
Publications: Art Bulletin (illustrated quarterly newsletter devoted to books and scholarly articles about all periods of art history); *Art Journal* (quarterly magazine focusing on current critical and aesthetic issues in the visual arts).

DALLAS SOCIETY OF VISUAL COMMUNICATIONS
3530 Highmesa Drive
Dallas, Tex.   75234
(214) 241-2017

Founded 1957. Focuses on the interests and activities of all professionals involved in visual communications.

Member Benefits: Complimentary roster of members, updated annually; employment referral service; group life and health insurance.
Educational Programs: Scholarships and internships available for art students; monthly meetings to view work of communications specialists from around the country; student show and seminar whereby students exhibit their finest work produced in the classroom (during the seminar, students are also given tours of design studios and agencies in the Dallas area).
Competitions/Exhibitions: The Dallas Show, a juried advertising and design competition open to artists from an eight-state area; student show and seminar (see under Educational Programs); annual screening of Clio Award-winning commercials.

Conference: Job Fair, held each spring to permit college students throughout the country to present their portfolios to area design studios and advertising agencies.
Awards: Dick Sloan Memorial Foundation Award, offered annually to two students enabling them to serve as apprentices at the design studio or advertising agency of their choice; Padgett award, given annually to one student and consisting of a free trip to the Aspen Design Conference; Golden Egg Award, given annually to an individual who makes an extraordinary contribution to creative arts in the Dallas advertising community.

DESIGN MANAGEMENT INSTITUTE
621 Huntington Avenue
Boston, Mass.   02115
(617) 232-4496

Founded 1980. Affiliated with the Massachusetts College of Art, provides a forum for fostering, understanding, and communicating design management issues through research, educational programs, conferences, and seminars. Has developed a significant archive of information compiled from conferences, lectures, and presentations, on the function of design and the role of design management.

Member Benefit: Discounts on design publications.
Educational Programs: Seminars; program for emerging design managers.
Conferences: Annual meeting; joint conference between graphic designers and educators; conference tour of Japan.
Publication: Bimonthly newsletter.

GRAPHIC ARTISTS GUILD
30 East 20th Street
New York, N.Y.   10003
(212) 777-7353

Founded 1969. National organization with headquarters in New York City and chapters in California, Colorado, Georgia, Indiana, Massachusetts, and Vermont, each of which runs its own programs. Houses the Giolito Communications Center, a resource library for graphic artists that can be used by members and nonmembers and that eventually aims to include audio tapes of important meetings and videos of professional education courses and business practices. Recently conducted a study on art competitions and contests and developed a set of ethical guidelines for entry calls. Promotes artists' rights legislation. Organization includes Cartoonists Guild.

166

Member Benefits: Representation and negotiation; discounts on art supplies; accounting referral service; legal referral network; free copy of the *Graphic Artists Guild Handbook*; group insurance.
Educational Programs: Traveling education program; workshops on self-promotion.
Publications: Monthly newsletter; the *Graphic Artists Guild Handbook: Pricing and Ethical Guidelines* (biannual compendium of pricing, standards, and practices for the graphics industry).

INDUSTRIAL DESIGNERS SOCIETY OF AMERICA
1142 E. Walker Road
Great Falls, Va.   22066
(703) 759-0100

Founded 1965. Nonprofit organization of professionals who design products, equipment, transportation, environments, packages, and information systems. Offers design information, educational opportunities, and design recognition programs. Publishes statistical studies on various subjects. Provides guidance through its Ethics Advisory Council.

Member Benefit: Group insurance.
Educational Programs: Regularly scheduled workshops and seminars.
Conferences: National conference held each August that includes specialized case studies and demonstrations; district conference held each spring in five locations throughout the United States, with emphases on design discussions of members' work and visual presentations.
Awards: Industrial Design Excellence Awards.
Publications: Design Perspectives (monthly newsletter); *Innovation* (quarterly journal focusing on case studies of design research and practice); membership directory.

INTERNATIONAL COUNCIL OF GRAPHIC DESIGN ASSOCIATIONS
12 Blendon Terrace, Plumstead Common
London SE18 7RS, England

Founded 1962 to forge links among professional graphic design associations in all countries. Aims to act as a nonpolitical representative and advisory body for the graphic design profession; to raise the standards of graphic design internationally; to improve and expand the contribution of graphic design to a greater understanding among people everywhere; to further appreciation of the professional problems and achievements of graphic designers in all countries; to promote coopera-

167

tion and exchange of information, views, and research among designers and between design organizations and those in allied fields; to contribute to the development of the theory and practice of graphic design education and research; to coordinate and develop matters of professional practice and conduct; and to establish international standards and procedures. Houses an audiovisual library and archive of international slides, tapes, films, and printed matter concerned with graphic communication. Slides are available on loan and, in certain cases, may be purchased. An Education Working Group is responsible for documentation, information exchange, student projects, and international educational collaboration. Finally, the organization issues many publications, which fall into three categories: general distribution, restricted distribution, and professional documentation.

Competitions/Exhibitions: Wide range of competitions; exhibitions held in conjunction with every congress and conference (conducted biannually); two traveling exhibitions.
Conferences: Annual meetings that enable designers, students, and representatives of other disciplines from all parts of the world to meet, exchange information, and plan for the future.
Awards: ICOGRADA Phillips Biennial Award, an important development in the encouragement of design innovation and a strengthening of ICOGRADA's links with industry; the President's trophy, an award made at each general assembly for outstanding contributions to the work and aims of the organization.
Publications: Icographic (biannual review of international visual communication design); *Icographic, volume 2* (information tool, published in English, based on specific themes of major interest to designers, teachers, researchers, and students); *Directory of Magazines*; *World Design Sources Directory.*

NATIONAL CARTOONISTS SOCIETY
9 Ebony Court
Brooklyn, N.Y.   11229
(718) 743-6510

Founded 1946. Headquarters in New York City, with regional groups across the United States. Society aims to further the interests of individuals who work in the profession. The Milt Gross Fund assists cartoonists in financial distress.

Conference: Annual convention.
Awards: Reuben Awards granted every April to the outstanding cartoonist of the year; Silver Plaque award honors the best cartoonist in each of twelve categories.
Publications: The Cartoonist (monthly newsletter); *NCS Album* (174-page paperback with photographs, art samples, biographies, and list of Reuben Award winners; *Occupation and Educational Guide.*

NEW YORK ARTISTS EQUITY ASSOCIATION

32 Union Square East, Suite 1103
New York, N.Y.   10003
(212) 477-8295

Founded 1947. Nonprofit organization established as a nonpolitical group to advance the cultural, legislative, professional, and economic interests of painters, sculptors, and printmakers in the visual arts.

Member Benefits: Health and dental insurance; fine arts insurance; information service; legal advice; Artists' Welfare Fund providing needy artists with interest-free loans.
Educational Programs: Forums featuring timely topics related to art; visits to out-of-town museums.
Awards: Annual merit awards to outstanding artists.

THE ONE CLUB

3 West 18th Street
New York, N.Y.   10011
(212) 255-7070

Founded in 1975 to promote excellence in advertising copywriting and design.

Member Benefits: Use of comprehensive library of publications pertaining to the creative side of advertising; private career counseling sessions with senior advisory board members on concerns ranging from work relationships to salary problems; job placement service.
Educational Programs: Portfolio reviews, whereby at least ten creative directors offer criticism and advice; "portfolio marriages," involving the exchange of ideas among copywriters and art directors, who work together to organize successful portfolios; portfolio crash course for junior copywriters and art directors, a one-month (four-session) intensive workshop for members only; annual lecture series by creative teams that have won Gold Awards (awarded to art directors and copy writers for best creative advertising in print, radio, and television);

lectures and panel discussions for groupheads and creative directors.
Competitions/Exhibitions: The One Show, a competition and traveling exhibition available for screening around the country.
Publications: The One Show (annual).

SOCIETY OF CHILDREN'S BOOK WRITERS
P.O. Box 296, Mar Vista Station
Los Angeles, Calif.   90066
(818) 347-2849

Founded 1968. Professional organization for writers and illustrators of children's literature. Offers opportunities for manuscript exchange, workshops with well-known writers and illustrators, and publications to aid artists.

Conference: National conference held in Los Angeles every August.
Awards: Golden Kite Awards, presented to selected authors and illustrators of children's books who are members of the society; Don Freeman Memorial Grant-in-Aid awards, $1,000 grants to members working in the illustrated-book field.
Publication: The Bulletin (bimonthly newsletter).

SOCIETY OF ENVIRONMENTAL GRAPHICS DESIGNERS
47 Third Street
Cambridge, Mass.   02141
(617) 577-8255

Founded 1978. Nonprofit professional organization representing the interests of those engaged in the discipline of environmental graphics design (signage). Develops standards and guidelines for the profession.

Conferences: Annual regional conference; national conference held every August at Cranbrook Academy of Art, Bloomfield Hills, Michigan.
Publications: Sourcebooks (comprehensive guides to materials, techniques, fabricators, and manufacturers involved in the execution of environmental graphics programs).

SOCIETY OF GRAPHIC DESIGNERS OF CANADA (ONTARIO CHAPTER)

P.O. Box 813
Adelaide Street East Post Office
Toronto, Ontario
M5C 2K1 Canada
(416) 366-5646

Founded 1956. Chapters in British Columbia, Alberta, the National Capital Region, and Atlantic Canada, as well as Ontario. Members are practicing professional graphic designers, educators, administrators, and students. Objectives are to secure and maintain a defined, recognized, and competent body of graphic designers and to promote high standards of graphic design for the benefit of Canadian industry, commerce, public service, and education. Adopts and sets standards of professional conduct for members; offers a network of professional assistance; lobbies with federal government departments concerning issues such as taxation, education, and general advocacy of design; and liaises with the international design community. Education committee advised the Ministry of Colleges and Universities on graphic design curriculum content.

Educational Programs: Seminars; symposium on design education.
Competitions/Exhibitions: The Best of the 80s, competition of graphic and editorial design and print advertising in Canada, from which a slide set is made of winning entries.
Awards: Ontario Students Graphic Design Awards.
Publications: Scan (newsletter); catalog of winning entries from The Best of the 80s show; *Code of Ethics and Professional Conduct for Graphic Designers.*

SOCIETY OF ILLUSTRATORS

128 East 63d Street
New York, N.Y.   10021
(212) 838-2560

Founded 1901. Created to promote interest in the art of illustration, past, present, and future. Houses the Museum of American Illustration, with exhibitions of original contemporary and historic art. Members participate in many projects, exhibit in group shows, and have access to luncheon and bar facilities.

Educational Programs: Sketch class for local residents; studio sessions without instructors; semi-annual lecture series featuring top professionals.

Competitions/Exhibitions: Student scholarship exhibition, a juried show with over fifty thousand dollars in grants to students in college-level art programs; annual juried show of published and unpublished illustrations.
Publications: Annual of American Illustration (catalog of selected entries from the show); monthly newsletter; *American Illustrators at Work* series of video cassettes.

SOCIETY OF ILLUSTRATORS OF LOS ANGELES
5000 Van Nuys Boulevard, Suite 400
Sherman Oaks, Calif.   91403
(818) 784-0588

Founded 1953. Instrumental in founding the Graphic Artists Guild of Los Angeles, SILA functions jointly with that organization in a variety of activities.

Educational Programs: Monthly meetings with speakers to discuss various aspects of illustration; workshops in how to set a price for your work; portfolio reviews.
Competition/Exhibition: Illustration West, an annual show of jury-selected illustrative work from thirteen western states and Canada, which includes a special student category.
Publication: Medium (bimonthly newsletter).

SOCIETY OF PROFESSIONAL GRAPHIC ARTISTS
C/O William Werrbach Studios Inc.
534 Westlake Avenue N., Suite 260
Seattle, Wash.   98109
(206) 622-6282

Open to freelancers, this organization has been active in promoting business and professional ethics. Provides financial and organizational strength to help resolve issues and achieve goals of common interest. Offers guidelines on how to buy and sell graphic artwork. Holds monthly meetings and exhibition of members' work.

Publications: Portfolio One; Portfolio Two (showcases of work by members).

SOCIETY OF TYPOGRAPHIC ARTS
233 East Ontario, Suite 301
Chicago, Ill.   60611
(312) 787-2018

Founded 1927. National communications design organization offering professional, educational, and social resources to the design community, with the aim of

172

encouraging design excellence for the benefit of society as a whole.

Member Benefits: Legal referral; access to reference library; access to STA Creative Registry; free copies of STA publications; listing in annual membership directory; special group insurance.

Educational Programs: Tuition assistance grants awarded annually to design students of dean's list caliber; annual Design Education Conference for designers, design educators, and students; annual design student conference affording opportunities for group visits to Chicago design firms and advertising agencies and offering a forum on job-related issues of interest to the entry-level designer; Design Chicago, a continuing series of programs highlighting the history and role of design in that city; STA Seminars consisting of individual presentations and panel discussions; STA Workshops, regularly scheduled presentations and training sessions conducted by practitioners.

Conferences: STA conferences, one-day meetings addressing issues of importance to design and design practices; Annual Fall Conference, two-day meetings including presentations, panel discussions, and workshops.

Competitions/Exhibitions: STA 100 show, an annual juried international design competition from which the 100 best entries are selected for exhibition and publication; STA Chicago, an annual juried competition comprised exclusively of the work of Illinois designers; Trademarks USA2, a juried retrospective exhibit of graphic and corporate identity from 1964 to 1983, which travels throughout the United States; members' exhibits.

Publications: STA Bulletin (monthly newsletter); *STA 100* (annual catalog of winning entries from the STA 100 show); *The Design Journal* (annual that examines in depth an issue critical to design practice); *Trademarks USA2* (special issue of *The Design Journal*—a catalog of the winning entries from the Trademarks USA2 show); *Statements* (quarterly publication of interviews and articles of interest to members and to the design community as a whole); *Code of Ethics and Professional Conduct* (accepted standard of ethics and professional conduct for STA members); *Professional Papers* (items of interest, developed, compiled, and edited by STA for its members and the design community); annual membership directory.

TYPE DIRECTORS CLUB
60 East 42nd Street, Suite 1130
New York, N.Y.   10165
(212) 983-6042

Seeks to raise standards of typography, to aid in the
compilation and dissemination of knowledge concerning
the use of type and related materials, and to cooperate
with other organizations having similar aims and
purposes.

Educational Program: Monthly luncheon lectures by
practitioners and historians.
Competition/Exhibition: Annual international typography
competition in which winning entries are granted
awards. The related exhibition travels throughout North
and South America, Europe, and Japan.
Publications: Typography (annual of winning entries
from the competition); *Gutenberg and Family* (magazine
published three times per year).

UNIVERSITY AND COLLEGE DESIGNERS ASSOCIATION
2811 Mishawaka Avenue
South Bend, Ind.   46615
(219) 288-UCDA

Created to improve the stature and credibility of designers and art directors within the academic community.

Member Benefit: Job placement service.
Competition/Exhibition: Annual competition for design
excellence in work produced for educational institutions,
held in conjunction with conference (see below). Showcase for best in college and university publications.
Conference: Held annually with keynote speakers from
the design profession and academe. Seminars and workshops address new tools and techniques, professional
growth, industry trends, and ways the designer may re-
late to institutions of higher learning.
Publication: Designer (quarterly newsletter).

WESTERN ART DIRECTORS CLUB
P.O. Box 966
Palo Alto, Calif.   94302
(415) 995-7338

A professional organization for people working in the
communicating arts field, including art directors,
graphic designers, illustrators, photographers, production artists, printers, and typographers.

Educational Programs: Seminars and creative lunches featuring prominent speakers; scholarship program providing financial assistance to graphic art and design students in Bay Area colleges and universities.
Competitions/Exhibitions: Portfolio Show, a nonjuried exhibition of work by members; West Coast Show, an exhibit of graphic art judged by nationally recognized professionals and open to all artists on the West Coast and in Hawaii.
Publications: Studio (newsletter); annual membership roster.

WOMEN IN DESIGN/CHICAGO

400 West Madison Street, Suite 2400
Chicago, Ill.   60606
(312) 648-1874

Nonprofit professional organization that focuses on the goals and interests of designers, with a particular interest in raising the status of women in the design community. Membership enables participation in multidisciplinary programs that are not only geared toward the graphic design profession, but spotlight topics such as fashion design, architecture, jewelry design, and interior design.

Educational Programs dealing with a wide range of topics, such as computer graphics, taxes and law, calligraphy, Japanese design, book design, and design management.
Publications: DesignDirections (monthly newsletter); membership directory

WOMEN'S GRAPHIC CENTER

1727 North Spring Street
Los Angeles, Calif.   90012
(213) 222-2477

Founded 1973. Professionally equipped community access studio used by artists to create books, broadsides, posters, and postcards. The mission of WGC is to encourage production of multiple works to reach a wider audience. Provides instruction, access to equipment, and technical assistance. Supports experimentation and encourages exploration.

Publication: The Newsletter of the Woman's Building.

4.
GRADUATE
PROGRAMS

Although continuing education is always helpful, it is not imperative that an illustrator or graphic designer have postgraduate training. Graduate school is fine for those who feel a need to pursue a specific approach not taught in undergraduate courses or unavailable to them on the job. It is also necessary for those who would like to enter full-time teaching. For those who are interested in learning more, the following art schools, colleges, and universities offer graduate programs that award the Master of Fine Arts (M.F.A.) degree or other degrees, as noted. Write or call them for information.

INSTITUTIONS OFFERING GRADUATE DEGREES IN ILLUSTRATION

ACADEMY OF ART COLLEGE
Department of Illustration
540 Powell Street
San Francisco, Calif.   94108
(415) 673-4200

ART CENTER COLLEGE OF DESIGN
Illustration Department
Pasadena, Calif.   91103
(818) 584-5000

COLORADO STATE UNIVERSITY
College of Veterinary Medicine
and Biomedical Sciences
Department of Anatomy
Fort Collins, Colo.   80523
(303) 491-5895
(Offers M.S. in biomedical illustration)

EAST CAROLINA STATE UNIVERSITY
School of Art
Greenville, N.C.   27834
(919) 757-6563

GEORGIA STATE UNIVERSITY
College of Arts and Sciences
School of Art and Design
University Plaza
Atlanta, Ga.   30303-3083
(404) 658-2291

176

KENT STATE UNIVERSITY
School of Art
Kent, Ohio   44242
(216) 672-2192

RHODE ISLAND SCHOOL OF DESIGN
Division of Illustration and Photographic Studies
2 College Street, Box 1A
Providence, R.I.   02903
(401) 331-3511

SAVANNAH COLLEGE OF ART AND DESIGN
Graduate Program in Fine Arts
Savannah, Ga.   31401
(912) 238-2483

SCHOOL OF VISUAL ARTS
Department of Media Arts
M.F.A./Illustrator as Visual Journalist
209 East 23d Street
New York, N.Y.   10010
(212) 683-0600

SYRACUSE UNIVERSITY
College of Visual and Performing Arts
Department of Visual Communications
200 Crouse College
Syracuse, N.Y.   13210
(315) 423-1870

UNIVERSITY OF UTAH
College of Fine Arts
Department of Art
Salt Lake City, Utah   84112
(801) 581-8677

INSTITUTIONS OFFERING GRADUATE DEGREES IN GRAPHIC DESIGN

ACADEMY OF ART COLLEGE
Departments of Advertising
and Graphic Design
540 Powell Street
San Francisco, Calif.   94108
(415) 673-4200

ART CENTER COLLEGE OF DESIGN
Communication Design Department
Pasadena, Calif.   91103
(818) 584-5000

BOSTON UNIVERSITY
School for the Visual Arts
Boston, Mass.   02215
(617) 353-3371

CALIFORNIA STATE UNIVERSITY, LONG BEACH
Department of Art
Long Beach, Calif.   90840
(213) 498-4376

CALIFORNIA STATE UNIVERSITY, LOS ANGELES
Department of Art
Los Angeles, Calif.   90032
(213) 224-3521

CITY UNIVERSITY OF NEW YORK, CITY COLLEGE
Division of the Arts
Department of Art
New York, N.Y.   10031
(212) 690-4202

**CITY UNIVERSITY OF NEW YORK,
GRADUATE SCHOOL AND UNIVERSITY CENTER**
Program in Art History
New York, N.Y.   10036
(212) 790-4451
(Offers Ph.D. in graphic arts)

COLORADO STATE UNIVERSITY
Department of Art
Fort Collins, Colo.   80523
(303) 491-5895

CORNELL UNIVERSITY
College of Architecture, Art,
and Planning
Ithaca, N.Y.   14853
(607) 256-3558
(Offers M.F.A. in creative visual arts,
with option for graphic design study)

CRANBROOK ACADEMY OF ART

500 Lone Pine Road, Box 801
Bloomfield Hills, Mich.   48013
(313) 645-3303

EAST CAROLINA STATE UNIVERSITY

School of Art
Greenville, N.C.   27834
(919) 757-6563

EAST TENNESSEE STATE UNIVERSITY

Department of Art
Johnson City, Tenn.   37614
(615) 929-4247

EAST TEXAS STATE UNIVERSITY

Department of Journalism and Graphic Arts
Commerce, Tex.   75428
(214) 886-5239
(Offers M.S. in journalism and graphic arts)

GEORGIA STATE UNIVERSITY

College of Arts and Sciences
School of Art and Design
University Plaza
Atlanta, Ga.   30303-3083
(404) 658-2291

ILLINOIS INSTITUTE OF TECHNOLOGY

Institute of Design
Chicago, Ill.   60616
(312) 567-3250
(Offers M.S. in visual design)

ILLINOIS STATE UNIVERSITY

Department of Art
Normal, Ill.   61761
(309) 438-5621

INDIANA STATE UNIVERSITY

Department of Art
Terre Haute, Ind.   47809
(812) 237-3698

IOWA STATE UNIVERSITY

College of Design
Department of Art and Design
Ames, Iowa   50011

KENT STATE UNIVERSITY
School of Art
Program in Graphic Design
Kent, Ohio   44242
(216) 672-2192

LOUISIANA TECH UNIVERSITY
School of Art and Architecture
Department of Art
Ruston, La.   71272

MANKATO STATE UNIVERSITY
Department of Art
Mankato, Minn.   56001
(507) 389-6413
(Offers M.A. in graphic design)

MARYLAND INSTITUTE
College of Art
1300 Mt. Royal Avenue
Baltimore, Md.   21217
(301) 669-9200

MEMPHIS STATE UNIVERSITY
College of Communications and Fine Arts
Memphis, Tenn.   38152
(901) 454-2216

MIAMI UNIVERSITY
School of Fine Arts
Program in Graphic Design
Oxford, Ohio   45056

MICHIGAN STATE UNIVERSITY
Department of Art
East Lansing, Mich.   48824-1119
(517) 355-7610

NORTHERN ILLINOIS UNIVERSITY
College of Visual and Performing Arts
DeKalb, Ill.   60115
(815) 753-1473

NORTHERN MICHIGAN UNIVERSITY
Department of Art and Design
Marquette, Mich.   49855
(906) 227-2194

PENNSYLVANIA STATE UNIVERSITY

University Park Campus
School of Visual Arts
University Park, Pa.   16802
(814) 865-0444

PRATT INSTITUTE

Graduate Design Programs
200 Willoughby Avenue
Brooklyn, N.Y.   11205
(718) 686-3670

RHODE ISLAND SCHOOL OF DESIGN

Department of Graphic Design
2 College Street, Box 1A
Providence, R.I.   02903
(401) 331-3511

ROCHESTER INSTITUTE OF TECHNOLOGY

School of Art and Design
Rochester, N.Y.   14623
(716) 475-2634

SAN DIEGO STATE UNIVERSITY

Department of Art
College of Professional Studies and Fine Arts
San Diego, Calif.   92182
(619) 265-6511

SAVANNAH COLLEGE OF ART AND DESIGN

Graduate Program in Fine Arts
Savannah, Ga.   31401
(912) 238-2483

SCHOOL OF THE ART INSTITUTE OF CHICAGO

Department of Design and Communication
Program in Visual Communication
Chicago, Ill.   60603
(312) 443-3700

SOUTHERN MASSACHUSETTS UNIVERSITY

Graduate School
College of Visual and Performing Arts
North Dartmouth, Mass.   02747
(617) 999-8000

STANFORD UNIVERSITY
Department of Art
Stanford, Calif.   94305
(415) 497-3404

SYRACUSE UNIVERSITY
College of Visual and Performing Arts
Department of Visual Communications
200 Crouse College
Syracuse, N.Y.   13210
(315) 423-1870

TEMPLE UNIVERSITY
Tyler School of Art
Beech and Penrose Avenues
Elkins Park, Pa.   19126
(215) 224-7575

UNIVERSITY OF ILLINOIS AT CHICAGO
School of Art and Design, Box 4348
Chicago, Ill.   60680
(312) 966-3337

UNIVERSITY OF ILLINOIS AT URBANA-CHAMPAIGN
School of Art and Design
Program in Graphic Design
Urbana, Ill.   61801
(301) 625-3286

UNIVERSITY OF KANSAS
School of Fine Arts
Department of Design
Lawrence, Kans.   66045
(913) 864-4401

UNIVERSITY OF MICHIGAN
School of Art
Program in Graphic Design
2000 Bonisteel Boulevard
Ann Arbor, Mich.   48109
(313) 764-0397

UNIVERSITY OF MISSOURI-KANSAS CITY
Department of Art and Art History
Program in Studio Art
Kansas City, Mo.   64110
(816) 276-1501
(Offers M.A. in graphic design)

UNIVERSITY OF UTAH
College of Fine Arts
Department of Art
Salt Lake City, Utah   84112
(801) 581-8677

UNIVERSITY OF WASHINGTON
College of Arts and Sciences
School of Art
Program in Graphic Design
Seattle, Wash.   98195

VIRGINIA COMMONWEALTH UNIVERSITY
School of the Arts
Department of Visual Communication Art and Design
325 N. Harrison Street
Richmond, Va.   23284
(804) 257-1700

YALE UNIVERSITY
School of Art
Department of Graphic Design
180 York Street
New Haven, Conn.   06520
(203) 436-4380

BIBLIOGRAPHY

The following list suggests some of the most valuable books on illustration, graphic design, and graphic art, both in and out of print. If you cannot find them in your bookstore, ask the bookseller to order them. If they are out of print, contact the publishing house directly or ask your local second-hand dealer to find them for you. Or, if you simply want to borrow, check your local library. Librarians will gladly make a computer search on an out-of-print book and borrow it for you from another library.

American Institute of Graphic Arts. *AIGA Four: Graphic Design U.S.A.* The Annual of the American Institute of Graphic Arts Series. New York: Watson-Guptill, 1983.

———. *AIGA Graphic Design U.S.A.* The Annual of the American Graphic Arts Series. New York: Watson-Guptill, 1985.

Appelbaum, Stanley, ed. *Scenes from the Nineteenth-Century Stage in Advertising Woodcuts.* New York: Dover, 1977.

Art Direction Magazine Editors. *Art for Commerce.* New York: Art Direction, 1974.

———. *Creativity.* Creativity Series, vol. 1. New York: Art Direction, 1972.

———. *Creativity, Four.* New York: Art Direction, 1975.

Art Directors Club of New York. *Sixty-second Art Directors Annual.* New York: Art Directors Club, 1983.

Ballinger, Raymond A. *Layout and Graphic Design.* New York: Van Nostrand Reinhold, 1970.

———. *Art and Reproduction: Graphic Reproduction Techniques.* Van Nostrand Reinhold, 1977.

———. *Designs with Paper in Art and Graphic Design.* New York: Van Nostrand Reinhold, 1982.

Barron, Don, ed. *Creativity.* Creativity Series, vol. 7. New York: Art Direction, 1978.

Barron, Don, and Art Direction Staff, eds. *Creativity.* Creativity Series, vol. 8. New York: Art Direction, 1979.

Baumgartner, Victor. *Graphic Games: From Pattern to Composition.* Englewood Cliffs, N.J.: Prentice-Hall, 1983.

Berryman, Gregg. *Notes on Graphic Design.* 2d edition. Los Altos, Calif.: W. Kaufman, 1983.

———. *Notes on Graphic Design and Visual Communi-*

cation. Rev. edition. Los Altos, Calif.: W. Kaufman, 1983.

Bertin, Jacques. *Semiology of Graphics.* Translated by William Berg. Madison, Wis.: University of Wisconsin Press, 1983.

Bettmann, Otto. *Bettmann Portable Archive.* New York: Picture House Press, 1966.

Bewick, Thomas. *Bewick's Woodcuts.* London: L. Reeve, 1870.

Blanchard, Russel W. *Graphic Design.* Englewood Cliffs, N.J.: Prentice-Hall, 1984.

Blechman, R. O. *R. O. Blechman: Behind the Lines.* New York: Hudson Hills Press, 1980.

Brunner, Felix. *A Handbook of Graphic Reproduction Processes.* Natick, Mass.: Alphabet MA, 1986.

Caplan, Ralph. *Graphic Packaging Four.* New York: Watson-Guptill, 1984.

Cardamone, Tom. *Advertising Agency and Studio Skills.* New York: Watson-Guptill, 1981.

⸻. *Mechanical Color Separation Skills for the Commercial Artist.* New York: Van Nostrand Reinhold, 1980.

Carter, Rob, et al. *Typographic Design: Form and Communications.* New York: Van Nostrand Reinhold, 1985.

Cheskin, Louis. *Color for Profit.* New York: Liveright, 1951.

Chwast, Seymour. *The Left Handed Designer.* Edited by Steven Heller. New York: Harry N. Abrams, 1985.

Click, John W., and N. Baird Russell. *Magazine Editing and Production.* Dubuque, Iowa: Wm. C. Brown, 1983.

Copperud, Roy H., and Roy Paul Nelson. *Editing the News.* Dubuque, Iowa: Wm. C. Brown, 1983.

Cordy, Peter, ed. *Creative Source.* 6th edition. New York: Robert Silver Associates, 1985.

Craig, James. *Designing with Type.* Edited by Susan Meyer. New York: Watson-Guptill, 1980.

⸻. *Graphic Design Career Guide: How to Get a Job and Establish a Career in Design.* New York: Watson-Guptill, 1983.

Crawford, Tad, and Arie Kopelman. *Selling Your Graphic Design and Illustration.* New York: St. Martin's Press, 1981.

Davis, Alex. *Package and Print: the Development of Container and Label Design.* New York: C. N. Potter, 1968.

Dictionary for the Graphic Arts: German-English, English-German. Old Tappan, N.J.: Perfect Graphic Arts, 1979.

Dictionary for the Graphic Arts in Eight Languages: German-English-French-Spanish-Russian-Hungarian-Polish-Slovak. Old Tappan, N.J.: Perfect Graphic Arts, 1979.

DiLemme, Phillip. *American Streamline: Handbook of Neon Advertising Design.* New York: Van Nostrand Reinhold, 1984.

Eastman Kodak. *Basic Color for the Graphic Arts.* Rochester, N.Y.: Eastman Kodak, 1981.

Estrin, Michael. *Two Thousand Designs, Forms and Ornaments.* New York: William Penn, 1947.

Fox, Charles P. *American Circus Posters in Full Color.* New York: Dover, 1978.

Gadney, Alan. *How to Enter and Win Design and Commercial Art Contests.* New York: Facts on File, 1982.

Gales, David. *Graphic Design Studio Procedures.* Monroe, N.Y.: Library Research Associates, 1982.

Garrett, Lillian. *Visual Design: A Problem-Solving Approach.* Melbourne, Fla.: Krieger, 1975.

Gatti, David. *Ready-to-Use Sale Announcements.* New York: Dover, 1980.

Gawain, Shakti. *Creative Visualization.* New York: Bantam, 1982.

Gill, Bob. *All the Rules You Ever Learned About Graphic Design: Including the Ones in This Book.* New York: Watson-Guptill, 1985.

Glaser, Milton. *Milton Glaser: Graphic Design.* New York: Overlook Press, 1973.

Gluck, Felix, ed. *Modern Publicity.* Vol. 48. New York: Macmillan, 1979.

Gottschall, Edward M. *Graphic Communication Eighties.* Englewood Cliffs, N.J.: Prentice-Hall, 1981.

Grafton, Carol B., ed. *Pictorial Archive of Decorative and Illustrative Mortised Cuts: Five Hundred and Fifty-One Eye-Catching Designs for Advertising and Other Uses.* New York: Dover, 1984.

Graphic Artists Guild. *Corporate and Communications Design Annual.* New York: Annuals, 1984.

————. *The Graphic Artists Guild Directory Four.* New York: Annuals, 1984.

Graphic Design International. Natick, Mass.: Alphabet MA, 1986.

Graphics Arts Trade Journals International. *Export Graphics U.S.A., 1983–84.* Edited by Lydia Miura et al. New York: Graphic Arts Trade, 1983.

Gray, Bill. *More Studio Tips for Artists and Graphic Designers.* New York: Van Nostrand Reinhold, 1978.

Halas, John. *Graphics in Motion.* New York: Van Nostrand Reinhold, 1984.

Harling, Robert, ed. *Alphabet and Image: A Quarterly of Typography and Graphic Arts.* 2 vols, nos. 1–8. Reprint of 1946 edition. Salem, N.H.: Ayer, 1975.

Harter, Jim. *Harter's Pictorial Archive for Collage and Illustration: Over 300 Nineteenth-Century Cuts.* New York: Dover, 1978.

Hartmann, Robert. *Graphics for Designers.* Ames, Iowa: University of Iowa Press, 1976.

Haskett, Mark S. *Design Your Own Logo: A Step-by-Step Guide for Businesses, Organizations, and Individuals.* Blue Ridge Summit, Pa.: TAB, 1984.

Hatton, Richard G. *Handbook of Plant and Floral Ornament.* New York: Dover, 1960.

Heal, Ambrose. *Sign-boards of Old London Shops.* London: B. T. Batsford, 1947.

Hechtlinger, Adelaide. *The Great Patent Medicine Era; or, Without Benefit of Doctor.* New York: Grosset and Dunlap, 1970.

Heller, Steven. *Innovators of American Illustration.* New York: Van Nostrand Reinhold, 1986.

———. *Man Bites Man: Two Decades of Satiric Art.* New York: A & W Publishers, 1981.

Henrion, F. H. *Top Graphic Design.* Natick, Mass.: Alphabet MA, 1986.

Henton, Richard W. *Quick-Sketch: A New Technique in Interior Design Graphics.* Dubuque, Iowa: Kendall-Hunt, 1980.

Herdeg, Walter. *Graphis Annual 1982–83: International Annual of Advertising and Editorial Graphics.* New York: Hastings, 1982.

———. *Graphis Posters Eighty-six: The International Annual of Poster Art.* New York: Watson-Guptill, 1986.

Hinwood, Tony. *Advertising Art.* Newton-Abbot, England: David & Charles, n.d.

———. *Graphics Ad Lib Number 3.* 2d edition. Woodstock, N.Y.: Beekman, 1977.

Hird, Kenneth F. *Understanding Graphic Arts.* Cincinnati, Ohio: South-Western, 1982.

Hirth, Georg. *Picture Book of the Graphic Arts: Thirty-five Hundred Woodcuts, Etchings, and Engravings by the Masters, 1500–1800.* Translated by Elena Tanasescu. Reprint of 1881 edition. 6 vols. Salem, N.H.: Ayer, 1969.

Hofer, Philip. *Baroque Book of Illustration.* Cambridge, Mass.: Harvard University Press, 1951.

Hofmann, Armin. *Graphic Design Manual: Principles and Practice.* New York: Van Nostrand Reinhold, 1965.

Holland, D. K., comp. *Graphic Artists Guild Handbook: Pricing and Ethical Guidelines*. 5th edition. New York: Graphic Artists Guild, 1984.

Hornung, Clarence. *Handbook of Early Advertising Art*. 2 vols. 3d revised edition. New York: Dover, 1956.

————. *An Old-fashioned Christmas in Illustration and Decoration*. New York: Dover, 1975.

————. *Background Patterns, Textures and Tints*. New York: Dover, 1976.

Hornung, Clarence, and Fridolf Johnson. *Two Hundred Years of American Graphic Arts*. New York: Braziller, 1976.

Hulteng, John L., and Roy Paul Nelson. *The Fourth Estate: An Informal Appraisal of the News and Opinion Media*. New York: Harper & Row, 1983.

Humbert, Claude. *Ornamental Design: A Source-book with 1,000 Illustrations*. New York: Viking Press, 1970.

Hurlburt, Allen. *The Design Concept*. New York: Watson-Guptill, 1981.

————. *Layout*. New York: Watson-Guptill, 1977.

Hutchinson, Robert. *Eighteen Hundred Woodcuts by Thomas Bewick and His School*. New York: Dover, 1962.

Institute of Engineering, Australia. *Graphics '83*. Brookfield, Vermont: Brookfield, 1984.

International Publications Service. *Graphic Art in Japan, 1982–83*. Philadelphia: International Publications Service, 1982.

Jacobowitz, Ellen S., and George H. Marcus. *American Graphics: 1860 to 1940*. Philadelphia: Philadelphia Museum of Art, 1982.

Jankimowicz, Irena. *Contemporary Polish Graphic Art*. New York: W. S. Heinman, 1977.

Japan Graphic Designers Association. *Graphic Design in Japan*. 4 vols. New York: Kodansha International, 1982–84.

Jones, Sydney R. *Art and Publicity: Fine Printing and Design*. Reprint of 1925 edition. Darby, Pa.: Arden Library, 1978.

Karsnitz, John R. *Graphic Arts Technology*. Albany, N.Y.: Delmar, 1984.

Kemnitzer, Ronald B. *Rendering with Markers: Definitive Techniques for Designers, Illustrators and Architects*. New York: Watson-Guptill, 1983.

Kemper, Alfred M. *Presentation Drawings by American Architects*. New York: John Wiley, 1977.

Latimer, Henry C. *Preparing Art and Camera Copy for Printing: A Contemporary Procedures Technique for*

Mechanicals and Related Copy. New York: McGraw-Hill, 1977.

Ludlow, Norman H., Jr. *Clip Book Number Thirteen: The People and Things We Live With.* Rochester, N.Y.: N. H. Ludlow, 1981.

—————. *Clip Book Number Fourteen: Disabled People at Work and Play.* Rochester, N.Y.: N. H. Ludlow, 1981.

McMullan, James. *Revealing Illustrations.* New York: Watson-Guptill, 1981.

Magnus, Gunter H. *Dumont's Handbook for Graphic Artists: A Practical Introduction.* Woodbury, N.Y.: Barron's, 1984.

Marcus, Aaron. *Managing Facts and Concepts: Computer Graphics and Information from Graphics Designers' Perspective.* New York: Publishing Center for Cultural Research, 1983.

Marquand, Ed. *How to Prepare Your Portfolio: A Guide for Students and Professionals.* New York: Art Direction, 1981.

Maurello, S. Ralph. *Commercial Art Techniques.* New York: Leon Amiel.

Meder, J., and Ein Handbuck. *Dürer-Katalog.* Graphic Art Series, vol. 12. Reprint of 1932 edition. New York: Da Capo Press, 1971.

Meggs, Philip B. *History of Graphic Design.* New York: Van Nostrand Reinhold, 1983.

Menten, Theodore. *Ready-to-Use Banners.* New York: Dover, 1979.

Menten, Theodore, ed. *Advertising Art in the Art Deco Style.* New York: Dover, 1975.

Mintz, Patricia. *Dictionary of Graphic Arts Terms: A Communication Tool for People Who Buy Type and Printing.* New York: Van Nostrand Reinhold, 1981.

Muller, W., ed. *Dictionary of the Graphic Arts Industry.* New York: Elsevier, 1981.

Muller-Brockmann, Josef. *A History of Visual Communication.* 2d edition. New York: Hastings, 1981.

—————. *The Graphic Designer and His Design Problems.* Natick, Mass.: Alphabet MA, 1986.

Nelson, Roy Paul. *Publication Design.* 3d edition. Dubuque, Iowa: Wm. C. Brown, 1983.

Nelson, Roy P., and Byron Ferris. *Fell's Guide to Commercial Art.* Hollywood, Fla.: Frederick Fell, 1966.

One Show: Advertising's Best Print, Radio, T.V. Vol. 4. New York: American Showcase, 1983.

Pattison, Polly. *How to Design a Nameplate: A Guide for Art Directors and Editors.* Chicago: Ragan Communications, 1982.

Peterson, John, and Kenneth Hird. *Mathematics for the Graphic Arts Trade.* Cincinnati, Ohio: South-Western, 1985.

Porter, Tom, and Sue Goodman. *Manual of Graphic Techniques: For Architects, Graphic Designers and Artists, No. 3.* New York: Scribner's, 1983.

———. *Manual of Graphic Technique Four: For Architects, Graphic Designers, and Artists.* New York: Scribner's, 1984.

Porter, Tom, and Robert Greenstreet. *Manual of Graphic Techniques.* New York: Scribner's, 1980.

Print Casebooks. 6 vols. 5th ed. Bethesda, Md.: R. C. Publications, 1986.

Printing Trades Blue Book: Delaware Valley–Ohio Edition. New York: A. F. Lewis, 1983.

Printing Trades Blue Book: Southeastern Edition. New York: A. F. Lewis, 1983.

Rand, Paul. *Paul Rand: A Designer's Art.* New Haven, Conn.: Yale University Press, 1985.

Reinfeld, George. *Opportunities in Graphic Communications.* Chicago: National Textbook, 1983.

Resnick, Elizabeth. *Graphic Design: A Problem-Solving Approach to Visual Communication.* Englewood Cliffs, N.J.: Prentice-Hall, 1984.

Roth, Laszlo. *Display Design: An Introduction to the Art of Window Display.* Englewood Cliffs, N.J.: Prentice-Hall, 1983.

Rotzer, Willy, and Jacques N. Garamond. *Art and Graphics.* In English, French, and German. New York: Hastings, 1983.

———. *Art and Graphics.* Natick, Mass.: Alphabet MA, 1986.

Ruder, Emil. *Typography.* Natick, Mass.: Alphabet MA, 1986.

Rudman, Jack. *Graphic Arts Specialist.* Syosset, N.Y.: National Learning, 1987.

Sainton, Roger. *Art Nouveau Posters and Graphics.* New York: St. Martin's Press, 1984.

Sanders, Norman. *Photography for Graphic Designers.* New York: Publication Center for Cultural Research, 1979.

Sanders, Norman, and William Bevington. *Graphic Designer's Production Handbook.* New York: Hastings, 1982.

Schad, Tennyson, and Ira Shapiro, eds. *Corporate Showcase.* Vol. 2. New York: American Showcase, 1983.

Schlemmer, Richard M. *Handbook of Advertising Art Production.* 3d edition. Englewood Cliffs, N.J.: Prentice-Hall, 1984.

Schmid, Calvin F., and Stanton E. Schmid. *Handbook of Graphic Presentation.* 2d edition. New York: John Wiley, 1979.

Schmittel, Wolfgang. *Process Visual: The Development of Corporate Visibility.* Natick, Mass.: Alphabet MA, 1986.

Sherbow, Benjamin. *Effective Type-use for Advertising.* Reprint of 1922 edition. Darby, Pa.: Arden Library, 1978.

Signs of the Times: Encyclopedia of 7,700 Illustrations. Garland, Texas: Assurance Publishers, 1979.

Silver, Gerald. *Graphic Layout and Design.* Albany, N.Y.: Delmar, 1981.

Smith, Virginia. *Alphagraphics.* New York: Scribner's, 1978.

Snyder, Gertrude, and Alan Peckulick. *Herb Lubalin: Art Director, Graphic Designer and Typographer.* New York: American Showcase, 1985.

Snyder, John. *Commercial Artists Handbook.* New York: Watson-Guptill, 1973.

Solo, Dan X. *Special Effects and Topical Alphabets.* New York: Dover, 1978.

Spence, William P., and David G. Vequist. *Graphic Reproduction.* New York: Scribner's, 1981.

Spurgeon, C. H. *The Art of Illustration.* Reprint of nineteenth-century edition. Pasadena, Texas: Pilgrim, 1971.

Stern, Edward L. *Printing and Graphic Arts Buyers Directory.* Hewlett, N.Y.: Hilary House Publishers, 1984.

Stevens, Peter S. *A Handbook of Regular Patterns: An Introduction to Symmetry in Two Dimensions.* Cambridge, Mass.: MIT Press, 1981.

Stevenson, George A. *Graphic Arts Encyclopedia.* 2d edition. New York: McGraw-Hill, 1979.

Strauss, Victor. *Graphic Arts Management.* New York: R. R. Bowker, 1973.

Sutphen, Richard. *The Encyclopedia of Small Spot Engravings.* Phoenix: Valley of the Sun, 1969.

Swerdlow, R. *Basic Book of Graphic Arts.* Homewood, Ill.: American Technical, 1979.

————. *Introduction to Graphic Arts.* Homewood, Ill.: American Technical, 1979.

Tax Planning for Your Graphic Arts Business. Arlington, Va.: Print Industries of America, n.d.

Thoma, Marta. *Graphic Illustration: Tools and Techniques for Beginning Illustrators.* Englewood Cliffs, N.J.: Prentice-Hall, 1982.

Tuer, Andrew White. *One Thousand Quaint Cuts.* New York: Art Direction, 1976.

Turnbull, Arthur T., and Russell N. Baird. *The Graphics of Communication: Typography, Layout, Design, Production.* 4th edition. New York: Holt, Rinehart and Winston, 1980.

Vries, Leonard de. *Victorian Advertisements.* London: Murray, 1968.

Wadsworth, John W. *Designs from Plant Forms.* New York: Universe, 1977.

Walker, John R. *Graphic Arts Fundamentals.* South Holland, Ill.: Goodheart-Willcox, 1980.

Weitenkampf, Frank. *American Graphic Art.* Reprint of 1924 edition. New York: Johnson Reprint, 1970.

White, Jan V. *Editing by Design: A Guide to Effective Word-and-Picture Communication for Editors and Designers.* 2d edition. New York: R. R. Bowker, 1982.

————. *Mastering Graphics: Design and Production Made Easy.* New York: R. R. Bowker, 1983.

————. *On Graphics: Tips for Editors.* Chicago: Ragan Communications, 1981.

Wileman, Ralph E. *Exercises in Visual Thinking.* New York: Hastings, 1980.

Wimer, Arthur, and Dale Brix. *Workbook for Head Writing and News Editing.* 5th edition. Dubuque, Iowa: Wm. C. Brown, 1983.

Zelanski, Paul, and Mary P. Fisher. *Design Principles and Problems.* New York: Holt, Rinehart and Winston, 1984.

INDEX